CW00820957

CARP SENSE

CARP SENSE

JIM GIBBINSON

Beekay Publishers

Other carp fishing titles by Beekay Publishers

CARP FEVER by Kevin Maddocks
BEEKAY GUIDE TO 1500 CARP WATERS by K Maddocks and P Mohan
MY PASSION FOR CARP by Andy Little
CARP (SAS SERIES) by Rob Maylin
CARP STRIKES BACK by Rod Hutchinson
CARP: NOW & THEN by Rod Hutchinson
CYPRY THE CARP by Peter Mohan
IN PURSUIT OF CARP & CATFISH by Kevin Maddocks
REDMIRE POOL by K Clifford & L Arbery
RITCHIE ON CARP by Ritchie McDonald
TIGER BAY by Rob Maylin
BEEKAY GUIDE TO CARP BAITS by K Maddocks & P Mohan
BIG-WATER CARP by Jim Gibbinson

First published in 1992
©BEEKAY PUBLISHERS
WITHY POOL
BEDFORD ROAD
HENLOW CAMP
BEDS SG16 6EA
ENGLAND

ISBN 0 947674 42

Typeset by BP Integraphics Ltd., Bath, Avon
Printed in Great Britain by The Bath Press, Bath, Avon

About the Author

Jim Gibbinson has fished for carp for more than 30 years. He has fished in innumerable waters in many different parts of the country and, in recent years, has extended his experience to France, Belgium and the Netherlands.

Early in his career he developed a particular love for big gravel-pits; they remain his preferred waters to this day, especially if they are lightly fished and contain previously uncaught carp. His most recent carp book, *Big-Water Carp*, concentrated on such places.

He has long since lost count of how many double-figure carp he has caught, and quite genuinely has no idea how many twenty-pounders he has taken either. His biggest carp are a 32½ lb common and a 31¼ lb mirror.

Although known primarily as a carp angler, he has had considerable success with other species, including what is probably the most notable catch of big pike ever taken in his home county of Kent, which comprised four over 25 lb from three different waters, taken in less than 24 hours!

He has also had remarkable success with tench, having taken upwards of 50 over 7 lb, topped by seven over 8 lb. His latest book *Tench* has received much acclaim.

He earns his living as a teacher—a job chosen because it gave him the maximum time to go fishing!

He is married with two sons and lives in Kent.

Acknowledgements

My thanks to my many friends who have handled cameras and landing-nets with equal expertise; and who have enriched my fishing with conversation, companionship, humour, information, trust and, where appropriate, water access and hospitality.

My gratitude also to Maria, who tolerates with equanimity my bait-making, my anti-social hours, my disappearances to the continent; and who suggested the title of this book.

Contents

Drawings by the author. Photos by the author and friends.
Front cover: A gleaming, almost certainly previously uncaught 24½ lb mirror
Back cover: Dennis plays a winter fish at sunset

Introduction

This, my fourth book on carp fishing, is intended primarily for experienced anglers. I have not attempted to produce an A to Z complete guide; so beginners might be frustrated by the fact that certain things are not comprehensively explained. Conversely, I expect some successful anglers will feel that I have, at times, laboured the obvious. Striking the correct balance is very difficult.

My most recent carp book, *Big-Water Carp*, was published in 1989 by Beekay, but this is by no means a "Son Of BWC"; a lot of the information is new and, with just one exception, all the carp pictures, and most of the other photos, are new too.

Although mainly concerned with carp fishing in UK, this book acknowledges that many anglers, myself included, do a significant proportion of our fishing on the continent. The scope of the book therefore extends to the sort of waters found in mainland Europe.

Its title, Carp Sense, is meant to convey the idea that it is about commonsense methods, approach and attitudes. And although it may sound like a pretentious thing to say, I hope it will help redress the balance as regards values, and offset the beer-and-curry ethos that carp fishing has recently acquired.

I cannot bring myself to fish waters that have been defaced and vandalised by ugly dug-outs, or where the lake's perimeter is scarred by grassless banks, bivvies, and litter—and where the sound of a mallet is more common than that of the skylark.

There is far more to carp fishing than "setting up the bivvy-home, and banging out the boilies". Successful anglers are always naturalists at heart; they try hard to understand how carp behave and respond to changes in their environment. Certainly techniques are important, and I have discussed rigs and tactics in detail. Baits are important too, and they get extensive coverage. But consistent success requires something beyond the rigs-and-baits syndrome; and I hope that comes through.

I do not fish the pressured "circuit-waters", so I have not attempted to describe how to catch carp that have probably been caught too often already. In these pages you will find no advice relating directly to the

The front-cover picture—a beautiful, gleaming never-been-caught-before 24½ lb mirror.

No dug-out to fish from, just a lovely grassy bank—and not another angler in sight.
My concept of real carp fishing.

capture of the "Parrots", "Nelsons" or "Beakies", that are so many
anglers' personal bests. If that is your sort of carp fishing, then I have
to tell you that you are reading the wrong author.

I suspect that what I have to say will probably find most favour
with those who do not think carp fishing is solely about catching twenties
and thirties. Yes, we all want to catch big fish, of course we do, and
I have been fortunate enough to catch my share; but merit cannot be
measured in pounds and ounces, and enjoyment cannot be weighed.

If you sympathise with that view, read on. If not—I suggest you
put the book back on the shelf. It is not for you!

1 Tackle and Equipment

Before I discuss the tackle and equipment I use, I would like to make the point that I have no commercial tie-ups; I obtain gear by the same means as you, with wonder-wallet-filler! So my recommendations are completely unbiased and are based solely on merit.

RODS

There are a lot of good rods available these days; they come in all price ranges too. To an extent you get what you pay for in that higher-priced rods are usually made from better materials (or materials that are subject to more stringent quality-control, which is not necessarily the same thing), and they generally come equipped with better fittings. But the more expensive rod might not necessarily have a better action or be a better fishing-tool. Likes and dislikes influence choice too. Take the example of some prototype long-range rods that a friend invited me to try. He was involved in their development and was understandably enthusiastic about them. Certainly they were superbly finished and were equipped with top-quality fittings. From discussions with him I knew too that the very best high-tech materials had been used in the construction of the blanks; but I did not like them at all. They were top-heavy and far too "brutish" for my taste.

Although I currently have no tie-up with any manufacturer, I did for several years have a consultancy contract with Tri-Cast. We parted company about three years ago, but I still use their rods. My favourite is the Diamond-Kevlar 12ft/2¼ lb model which is designated M/L 7–14; which indicates that it is best suited for medium to long-range fishing with lines of from seven to 14lb test. Although specifically designed for medium to long-range fishing, and will put a two and a half ounce lead well beyond the 100yd mark, it is forgiving enough to use in close-range situations. It is also a beautiful rod on which to play fish; the general balance and feel is nice too. I have yet to handle a rod I like better.

I have the 11 ft version too, and this is my choice when I am fishing

Footnote: Since writing these comments I have become involved with the development of a new range of carp rods with Simpsons of Turnford.

waters with high, steep banks, or where there are a lot of overhanging trees—situations where a 12 ft rod can be a bit of an encumbrance.

A number of tackle-dealers offer a custom-service and will make up rods on blanks of your choice, with any fittings you care to choose; so it might be helpful if I give quite precise details:

Blank	12 ft/2¼ lb fast-taper Diamond Kevlar
Rings	5 sides, Seymo GHI/E: 20 mm, 15 mm, 12.5 mm, 10 mm and 7 mm.
Ring-spacing	11 in, 12 in, 15 in, 18 in, 24 in
Tip	5 mm Fuji SiC PST: 2.8 mm barrel
Winch-fitting	FPS 18 mm (positioned so reel stem is 24½ in from end of blank)
Grips	3 × 5 in Duplon torpedo plus button or cap on butt-end

Blank	11 ft/2¼ lb fast-taper
Ring spacing	10 in, 12 in, 15 in, 18 in, 21 in

All other details as per 12 ft model

For really long-range, my choice is Tri-Cast's 12 ft/2 lb 10 oz E/R (Extreme Range) 6–15 model. This will cast a three ounce bomb a long, long way.

Long-range rods need to be properly ringed for the purpose and the best rings, without doubt, are Fuji silicon-carbide SVSG sides and PST tip. These are well made, very high quality rings, but a set of four sides and one tip (the ideal number for a 12 ft long-range rod) comprising 30 mm, 20 mm, 12 mm and 8 mm plus tip, will come to a cool £30, give or take a few pence—they are worth it though.

Ring spacing for these long-range rods incidentally, is: 12 in, 17 in, 22½ in, 28 in.

This places the large diameter butt-ring about 37 in above the top of the reel-fitting.

REELS

Despite the vast array of reels on the market these days, few qualify as perfect. Perhaps I am fussier than most, because over the years I have not shared contemporary enthusiasm for most of the models that have enjoyed periods of fashionable popularity. Among the commonest faults were poor angle of attack to the line-roller, so the line wore against the pick-up bracket, poor line-lay, inadequate spool-length, too great a distance from reel-seat to spool-lip, thus making it difficult to "feather" the cast, premature pick-up closure resulting in mid-air snap-offs (danger-

My current usual set-up: Tri-cast 2¼ lb 12 footers, Daiwa TD2050S reels, mini-alarms, Swingers and "pod".

ous as well as a nuisance), jerky clutch mechanisms, fiddly anti-reverse operation, poor reliability, erratic after-sales back-up ... I could go on. I am, however, delighted to say that I have now found perfection ... twice over. Two years ago I bought three of the then new Shimano Aero 4000X; and a few months later three Daiwa TD2050S. Neither model has a bait-runner facility, but can be used bait-runner style by the simple expedient of fishing with a very loose clutch. This "clutch-runner" style, as I call it, was demonstrated to me by a couple of French friends, the Mahin brothers; who between them have caught more big carp than most of us can ever hope to see ... for example, how does twenty, twenties in a day sound? No, that was not a misprint. ... They use Daiwa beachcasting reels of a type that I have not seen in UK; but any reel with a smooth and reliable clutch may be used, providing it slackens off to virtual free-spool, and can be turned to carp-playing-mode with one revolution or so of the clutch-adjusting knob. It would not be such an efficient system if the knob had to be cranked round several times.

The spool of the Daiwa TD2050S is the same length as that of the Shimano 4000X, but is four millimetres less in diameter; which in practical terms means that the Daiwa spills about 6.75 in (170 mm) of line per coil, compared with the Shimano's 7.25 in (185 mm) per coil. That **just** gives the Shimano the edge when used with heavy lines, say over about 12 lb test, as line will drop marginally less from its slightly larger spool. Other differences are small. The Daiwa is a bit more compact, but their respective weights are almost identical at about 14.5 ounces; and although they have different gear ratios (4.7:1 for the Shimano and 5.2:1 for the Daiwa), they retrieve at an almost identical rate due to the Shimano's slightly larger spool. Both have perfect line-lay, ball-bearing smoothness, superb clutch systems and have proved to be completely reliable. I am delighted with them.

The clutch-runner system works fine in open water and when fishing at medium-range or beyond, but engagement can be just that bit too slow when fishing near weed or snags. Also initial clutch-adjustment with this method is somewhat imprecise, which is a liability when fishing the margins because a fast moving, powerful fish might be hooked on a clutch that is too slack to permit adequate control, or so severe as to risk a line break or hook pull. I therefore decided I needed some reels with a proper bait-runner facility so recently bought three Daiwa Bite-N-Run, BR 2050. Early indications are promising but I have not yet used them for a sufficient length of time to comment on their reliability.

LINE

Whatever brand of mono you use, remember that designated breaking-strains are only nominal and I recommend that you test every spool you buy and redesignate it. This also provides a safeguard against the odd rogue batch of line that breaks at a much lower breaking-strain than it should.

For nearly all my carp fishing I use 12 lb Berkley Big-Game line (which tests out at about 16 lb after a nine hour soak); 10 lb test for long-range light-line work; and 15 lb test (about 20 lb actual) for shock-leaders or for fishing near rocks, wooden piles and lock-gates.

Certainly its qualities of abrasion resistance are superior to any other line I have ever tried, which makes it ideal for the weedy gravel-pits on which I do most of my carp fishing; but as well as that, it is very, very nice line. It is smooth, supple, has low memory (does not remain in annoying coils when it comes off the spool) and knots well.

Talking of abrasion-resistance, I must mention Kryston's new Quick-Silver shock-leader braid. I have not used it for actual fishing, nor have I yet devised a neat, reliable knot for joining it to my main-line, but my bench-tests have convinced me that it is more abrasion-resistant than any other rubbing-leader material I have tried. I have great hopes for it and think it will probably be the answer to gravel-bar cut-offs.

A lot of anglers do not like uncoloured line and have persuaded Terry Eustace, who distributes Big Game Line in UK, to sell a sorrel version. I prefer the clear, because to my eyes it is the least conspicuous under water; but "invisibility" is not necessarily a virtue, as I recently discovered. When I was last with the aforementioned Mahin brothers; Michel gave me some startling looking fluorescent yellow line to try. The Mahins swore by it; but notwithstanding their amazing success, I was not convinced and it remained unused for more than a year. A couple of months ago I decided to load-up with it, and have discovered, to my considerable surprise, that I really like it! Apart from the fact that it is a supple, reliable line, it has the unexpected but considerable advantage that swans and other water birds do not swim into it. It scares the hell out of them, in fact! Even geese, which let us face it, have got to be the dimmest creatures on this earth, with an IQ somewhere between that of a plant and a wind-surfer, say about that of a jet-skier, swim round it! And it is a dream on which to play fish because you can see exactly where they are, even in the half-light of dawn and dusk. Whether or not it would scare carp I do not know, I have so far only used it with a shock-leader of 15 lb Berkley. Although in this connection it might be worth mentioning that number-two son, Peter, caught a lot of margin fish last summer on Siglon line which, although not imbued with the laser-like brightness of the French stuff, is quite a distinct yellow. Peter used it straight-through too.

On the subject of tackle-visibility and its effect on carp; Rick experimented with variously-coloured anti-tangle tube while fishing at Layer, and found that it made no discernible difference to his catches. That said, I like my rig-bits to be dull and flash-free.

HOOKS

My all-purpose carp-hook was for several years the Mustad O'Shaughnessy pattern 34021. Then three or four years ago Dave Merritt and Pete Springate introduced me to Owner spade-ends (as far as I know they are only obtainable from Middlesex Angling Centre). They proved to be superb for use in conjunction with lines up to about eight or nine pounds test, and so became my first-choice light-line hook; the Mustad still being my choice for heavier lines. Frankly I would have been completely happy with those two patterns had Peter Drennan not introduced his new Starpoint hooks. Like the Owner pattern, they are best suited to lines of up to about eight or nine pounds test. I liked them but because most of my fishing in recent seasons has been done in very weedy waters, I did not give them a proper trial. Rick, however, enjoyed some phenomenal winter success on his Essex waters and during the course of a 'phone call to tell me about the capture of a magnificent 28 lb mirror, unambiguously stated that in his opinion Starpoints were the best hooks in the universe! Given to muted enthusiasm is Rick! Peter Drennan subsequently told me that he plans to introduce a "whopper-stopper" version; and I heard from Dave Merritt that a super-strong eyed version of the Owner is being produced, with a newly developed point that the Japanese manufacturers claim is sharp enough to penetrate bone, will not dull, and is constructed in such a manner that it will not tear a carp's mouth. If Drennan's whopper-stopper Starpoint, or the new Owner comes up to expectations, it could just be a case of "move over Mustad"! Time will tell.

I have tested my chosen patterns and know with what breaking-strain lines they can be safely used; if you use different hooks, I earnestly recommend that you test them by rigging them on strong line and a spring-balance to see how much pull they withstand before distorting. You may find, for example, that a pattern claimed to be a "good snag-hook" might not be as strong as you suppose.

My chosen selection test-out as follows (the first figure shows when distortion becomes apparent; the second figure indicates when the degree of distortion is probably sufficient to result in a lost hook-hold):

Mustad 34021 size six: 8 lb/11 lb
Owner size seven: 6 lb/8 lb
Starpoint size six: 6 lb/8 lb

Those figures may be lower than you expected; but when you test your own favourite patterns, I think you will be even more surprised.

HOOK-LINK MATERIALS

The modern High Performance Polyethylene (HPPE) hook-link products are excellent. My favourites are Kryston's 15 lb test Merlin and Rod Hutchinson's 15 lb The Edge, because they sink and lay flat on the bottom. Kevin Nash's Gamabraid sinks too, but not quite as positively as do Merlin and The Edge. Most other HPPE braids are semi-buoyant, which can result in their rising in the water and creating a loop between bait and lead. I do not think this matters if pop-ups are being used, in fact I am not totally convinced that it matters at all, but I feel happier if the hook-link lays flat.

The nicest of the braids to handle is Kryston's 14 lb Super Silk. It is Rick's favourite, but some anglers are put off by the fact that it is white. My experiments suggest that it is no more visible than the other braids.

Footnote: I have since tried the new eyed Owners—they are excellent.

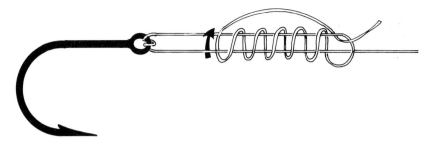

Fig. 1 My five-turn clinch-knot. An excellent knot for tying hooks and swivels to either HPPE braids or mono.

The toughest of them is Drennan Hi-Tenacity Braid. It is not as supple as the others, but it is less prone to damage and the 20 lb version is my first choice for fishing in thick weed.

Where hook-link abrasion is a serious problem, near rocks, piles and really bad gravel bars for example, I would use 25 lb test Kryston Quick-Silver.

I have spent hours experimenting with various knots in HPPE materials and have come to the conclusion that the best and safest knot is my five-turn clinch-knot. Although I have described it before; in the interests of completeness will show it again here (Fig 1). I always touch knots in HPPE with a tiny dab of Superglue—it gives added strength as well as security. With Superglued clinch-knots I find that I get **at least** the designated breaking-strains.

ALARMS AND INDICATORS

For the last three years I have been using some mini-alarms that a friend made for me. They are not generally available so there is little point in my giving further details. Of Vipers, Daiwa Sensitrons, Fox Microns and the new crop of Optonics I have no experience so cannot comment.

Alarms must fulfil two essential criteria: they must be reliable and weatherproof. My own preference is for an alarm that is not too sensitive —I do not want to have to suffer the irritation of buzzes and bleeps every time the wind gusts or a wave laps against the line. Some anglers go to great pains to render optical-sensor alarms super-sensitive by means of multi-vane beam-breakers. I feel neither the inclination nor the need for such refinement—but that said, I am not so naive as to assume that every time a carp touches my bait, my alarms register the fact. But frankly

Footnote: Del Romang has now brought out his long-awaited new alarms. Rick, who was involved in prototype tests, tells me they are superb.

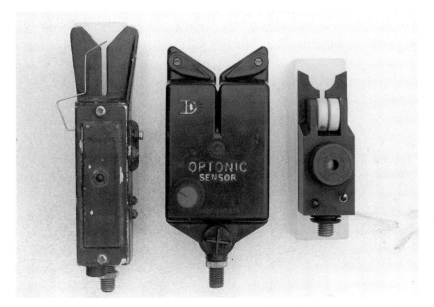

The three ages of alarms: converted Heron, converted Optonic, and my custom-made mini-model.

I cannot see the point of registering the sort of millimetric movement to which I would be completely incapable of responding anyway. My alarms give reliable indication of any lift or drop of more than an inch or so—and that is sensitive enough for my purposes.

I do not like wires trailing across my pitch, so prefer all-in-the-head alarms, or "compacts" as they are usually called.

Many modern alarms come in a choice of high or low tone. I prefer a high tone because it is a very penetrating note, even when not particularly loud; mine are easily heard above wind-noise and never fail to wake me if I am asleep. Some anglers always go to extremes though, and if high-tone alarms become the "in" thing to own, they will get higher and higher until only bats can hear them!

Not that low-tone alarms are without their disadvantages; ask Zen Bojko about the time he was awakened by a loud "quacking" sound but was puzzled because he couldn't see any ducks ... then realised it was one of his newly converted Optonics! I believe the story had a happy ending in the form of a 25 lb mirror.

Alarms seem to be getting louder these days. The other weekend I was fishing a very large pit and during the day heard what sounded

Fox "Swinger" indicator.

like a Klaxon. For a fleeting moment I wondered if there had been a gas or radiation leak from the nearby chemical works, but then realised that it was an angler on the opposite side of the pit adjusting his indicators! A quarter of a mile away for heaven's sake!

For clutch and bait-runner styles I use Fox Swingers. I think they are great; no more trying to get needles in rock-hard ground, and no more fiddling about with needle-bars. They are convenient when moving swims too, because they remain attached to the buzzer-bar.

On the rare occasions I fish running water, I use some special mega-heavy "monkeys"; but hardly ever use them otherwise.

SUNDRIES

Bank-sticks are important items—they need to be tough, durable, stable and practical. My choice is Chris Brown's bank-stick/buzzer-bar set; although I am not so sure about his latest version that has a nylon collar and adjusting-screw (mine are the old ones that have metal fittings). They are larger diameter than most, and this makes them less likely to turn; thus obviating the need for stabilisers. He produces a robust compatible rod-pod too, and having used it for a couple of seasons I have come

Rod-pod in use; in this instance on a canal. I have come to regard a "pod" as indispensable.

to realise just how indispensable it is. A lot of my fishing is done in gravel-pits where hard, stony banks can be virtually impenetrable; and a rod-pod is a much more sensible solution than a mallet ... a fact that has escaped those brain-dead morons who sabotage not only their own chances of success, but everyone else's as well, by battering hell out of the bank while setting up. Use of a mallet on quiet waters should be a hanging offence. At least!

Talking of bank-sticks and rod-rests; have you tried John Robert's new butt-grips? They are such simple little items, but so practical and efficient. They hold rods securely in high winds, or when violent takes occur; they also prevent rods from sliding if they are steeply angled. They really are excellent.

For seating I use a Fox bedchair. For a long while I balked at paying a hundred pounds or so for a bedchair when I could get a sun-bed for a fraction of the cost; but after demolishing my umpteenth sun-bed due to its designer self-destruct features, I capitulated and paid-out for a Fox model. I should have done it years ago—not only is it far stronger than the sun-bed, it is very much more comfortable. I recently made it even more comfortable by replacing the original canvas cover with a fully sprung padded mattress-cover which, as well as providing extra comfort, gives excellent underbody insulation from the cold.

I do not use a holdall to carry my rods, preferring to lash them made-up to my landing-net handle with some home-made Velcro/elastic rod-bands. Tip-sections are secured to butts with rod/lead bands, which prevent leads on terminal tackles damaging rods or rings.

I use a sling to carry bank-sticks, net, keep-sack, weigh-sling, throwing-stick, umbrella and, if necessary, storm-sides.

My other tackle items I carry in a back-packer's ruck-sack. Mine is designed on orthopaedic principles and is much easier to carry than are most fishing bags; but having said that, I have to concede that some of the newer carp-bags look very good and are undoubtedly a considerable improvement on their predecessors.

FUNCTION NOT FASHION!

Clothing must keep the angler warm, dry and comfortable. Most summer nights are adequately catered for with little more than a track-suit or similar, but damp autumn nights are another matter. Once we get into October and beyond, we need to think very seriously about what we wear because prolonged exposure to cold can be dangerous.

Thermal underwear comprising long-johns and a long-sleeved vest provides a sensible start. Most chain-stores sell these, especially if they have a ski-wear department. Next a track-suit or a quilted undersuit, and on top of that some padded bib-type trousers, a thick real-wool sweater and possibly a body-warmer.

Overtrousers will keep legs dry when it is wet, and the whole ensemble needs to be topped-off with a good quality warm, waterproof coat made from heavy-duty proofed nylon or, better still, one of the new wonder-fabrics which have the remarkable ability to permit sweat vapour to pass through, but will not allow rain to penetrate.

Fishing-clothing manufacturers have at last recognised the potential of these fabrics, and purpose-designed garments are now available, including superb one-piece suits which, worn over thermal underwear and a fleecy undersuit, will keep the wearer warm in temperatures way below freezing-point.

Footwear is a problem for some, but not for others, it depends if you suffer from cold feet. Moonboots are popular, but not all models are waterproof; a good alternative is a pair of ordinary wellies or waders bought at least two sizes too large. Worn with a pair of thick fleecy ski-boot socks in conjunction with a pair of over-large, woollen sea-boot socks, cold feet are not a problem.

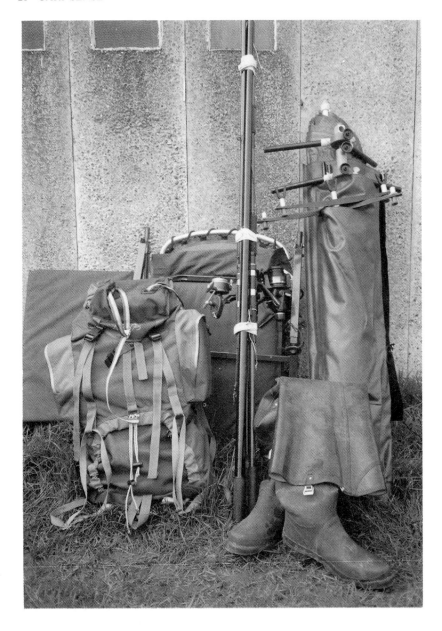

My usual range of equipment for all except overnight sessions: note unhooking-mat, rods bound to net-handle, and sling for brolly, bank-sticks and "pod".

A gale treats my 45 in brolly with disdain; Denis's 50 in model fares much better.

For short summer day-sessions I usually carry a 45 in umbrella, I do this even when the weather looks set fair because it serves as a sun-shade as well as a wind and rain shelter. It may not be adequate though, like the time a couple of years ago when Rick and I fished a Loire-Valley pit in an August heatwave. My main consideration in choosing a pitch was to select one beneath trees that afforded all-day shade! Poor Rick fished on the sunny side of the lake and was crisped despite sitting in the "shade" of his umbrella! Our final day was so hot that our trainers melted! Honest! Well, the adhesive holding them together did.

A 45 in model is not large enough for real wet and windy weather protection, especially at night (for, as everyone knows, night-time rain is wetter than daytime rain!); when a 50 in model is better. Protection from side-blown rain is afforded by storm-sides. An alternative that eliminates the need for storm-sides is an oval umbrella. These are extremely roomy and sit very low to the ground along their edges, thereby giving excellent side protection. Proofing is advisable, however, because although the fabric used for oval brollies is completely waterproof, untreated seams may drip in a downpour.

You will notice that I have made no mention of a bivvy; I never

I like Nashy's oval brolly for night sessions.

use one because I think they look ugly. I hate to see them dotted round a water like sprawling giant fungoid growths.

SURVIVE THE EXPERIENCE

An important item, or collection of items, that I always carry is a first-aid kit. Included in it are a few essentials that can make the difference between an enjoyable trip, and an uncomfortable or ruined one. My kit contains Paracetamol, plasters, sting/bite relief, anti-histamine tablets to prevent a wasp-sting from swelling, and diarrhoea-tablets. In summer I carry high-factor sun-screen and lip-protector. Sun-protection may not be a commonplace requirement in UK, but we get occasional broilers (remember 1990?). In France, of course, such conditions are commonplace. It is always a temptation for us pallid Brits to strip-off and lay in the sun whenever the opportunity arises, but it is unwise to do so. Apart from the risk of sunburn which, as we know, can lead to skin-cancer, it can result in sunstroke which, at best will make the sufferer feel very ill, and at worst can result in hospitalisation. I remember too when a friend of

It is a temptation to strip off and soak up the sun—but probably unwise.

mine sat out all day in the August sun on one of my local pits, and 24 hours later had the most horrible pair of swollen, pustulous lips you can imagine. So cover-up and stay in the shade.

I made brief mention then of sting/bite relief; but prevention, they say, is better than cure, so I always take some anti-mosquito cream or liquid. "Jungle Formula" is one of the better ones, but none are wholly effective for the simple reason that no matter how completely you endeavour to cover all biteable surfaces—mossies will find a way through somewhere. They will get inside your nostrils and inside your ears, along your parting and hairline; they will even attack your eyelids. God, they are **evil**! They have quite literally driven me to pack up on occasions, and there are waters that I will not fish of an evening in summer because they make life so unbearable.

Recently I have acquired a little gadget that looks like a lady's powder-puff case (mmmmm, nice!), but is actually an ultra-sonic mosquito repeller. It evidently mimics the sound of the amorous male mosquito which, in turn, is supposed to keep away pregnant females which, according to the literature accompanying the gadget, are the ones that bite. I am not convinced, but I reckon it is well worth the five pounds the gadget cost to find out. If it does work it will be the perfect answer because I am always reluctant to use creams etc in case their smell contaminates my bait. I have, however, an absurd image in my mind of the ultrasonic vibrations from the gadget working on carbon-fibre the way a certain pitch of human voice is supposed to react on glass—setting up a resonance that results in it shattering! Can you imagine; not a mossie in sight but three matched carbons lying in splinters at the water's edge!

Another item I will mention in this section, although it does not qualify as angling equipment in the literal sense of the phrase, is a camera. Most carp anglers carry one, so a few relevant comments might be helpful. Modern auto-focus, auto-exposure, auto-wind, auto-load ... in fact, auto-**everything** cameras, could have been designed with us in mind. They have their limitations though, and anyone who knows anything about photography will occasionally be frustrated by the lack of manual-override (eg, you want to photograph a sunset, and the knowall camera decides you need flash ...); but for most purposes they are superb. With care, excellent results can be achieved. I have a couple of Minolta compacts and a Canon, and their results are virtually indistinguishable from photos taken with my Olympus OMIN SLR models. But a few cautionary comments from one who has learned the hard way might help pitfalls be avoided:

1. Do not use a bank-stick/camera-adaptor arrangement to support the camera for self-take shots; the bank-stick will quiver and you will get blurred pictures. A tripod is best. Admittedly we carry quite enough equipment already without wanting to burden ourselves with extra photo-gear; but a lightweight tripod is a must if you want good pictures.

2. Non-zoom auto-compacts have a relatively wide-angle lens, which means you need to get far closer to the subject than you might expect. So no matter whether you are taking pictures, having pictures taken or setting-up for a self-take, **get in close**. I have lost count of the number of times the friend taking pictures for me has said, "I'll cut off your head if I don't move back," or, "I can't get all the fish's tail in the picture from here." I have given up trying to convince them otherwise and now let them go ahead according to their convictions; then I ask them to suppress their disbelief and move in closer—despite the risk of decapitation! The close shots **always** turn out best.

3. Auto-cameras tend to select slow shutter-speeds in poor light, which exacerbates the problem of camera-shake. So if I catch a fish in failing light I either sack it for a while, until the camera switches over to flash-mode, or I use a tripod. Flash-mode will give better colours.

Camera-shake is the main reason for blurred pictures—and a friend who can depress a shutter without moving the camera is a friend indeed. A lot of people instinctively "follow-through" when they press the shutter-

A tripod is essential for sharp self-take shots.

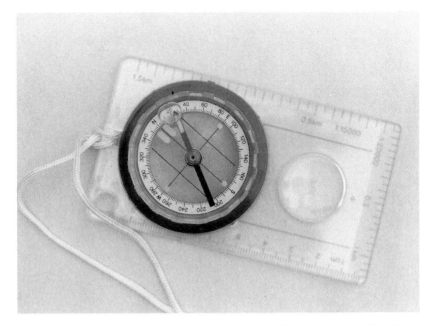

A pocket-compass is a useful item to help predict where forecasted winds will strike when arriving on a flat-calm dawn.

button—by that I mean that they move the camera in the same direction. Even in bright light and with a fast shutter-speed this will result in loss of crispness; while in poor light and with the consequent slow shutter-speed, the result will be a very blurred picture indeed.

Although I mentioned retaining fish in a sack for a while to wait for the light to change (I sometimes do it early in the morning too, to wait for the light to improve), most times I like to photograph carp immediately after unhooking. A carp that has just been caught will lay quiet and will generally cooperate while photos are being taken—but after a fish has had time to recover in a sack, particularly if it is a big one, it can take a bit of controlling. It is in the carp's best interest to photograph them immediately after landing and then release them without any period of retention.

Do not, incidentally, support a carp on your knee while holding it. At the point of knee-contact a carp has no ribs to protect its internal organs; and surely that must put the fish at risk of injury.

Never sack carp for more than a few minutes in high water temperatures. In very warm weather the margins can be denuded of oxygen and

Machined alloy torch—the **only** sort I have found to be completely reliable.

carp will die. A number of big fish have been lost this way in recent hot summers.

Cameras do not like the damp, nor do they like excessive heat; so carry them in a suitable waterproof container with a pack of silica-gel, and keep the camera-bag/box out of the sun. Do not let a camera bounce around in the boot or glove-compartment of a car either; they do not take kindly to vibration. I always carry mine on one of the seats, or on a pile of soft clothing.

Do not be tempted to use cheap film. Modern auto-compacts may be idiot-proof in that they require absolutely no knowledge of photography, but they are sophisticated bits of kit with very high quality optics, so they deserve top quality film. I recommend Fujichrome 100 or Kodachrome 64 . . . and a tripod!

I have saved the most important item till last; an unhooking-mat. Every carp angler should have one. Kevin Nash produces one for about £12; while up-market inflatable versions are available that cost about three times as much. Alternatively you might be able to scrounge a redundant baby's changing-mat from someone—they do not make these in jungle-green or matt-black, but does it really matter if it is covered with smiling ducks or a pretty floral pattern? Its sole purpose is to protect carp from underbody injury. So, no matter whether it is cheap, expensive or makeshift—get one. I think **every** angling club should make use of unhooking-mats compulsory.

And ban mallets!

2 Terminal Tackle

It always amuses me somewhat when I see features about various terminal tackles, because I know that the vast majority of those who write such pieces do most of their fishing with just one or two favourite, proven set-ups. Very sensible too. So why all those articles? It is because editors know that readers like them; so they continually ask their writers to come up with something new.

Now you know!

So this chapter will not contain details of my anti-eject sliding revolving wonder-rig with warp-drive! Believe me, most so called "sophisticated rigs" are no better than standard arrangements, and many are a lot worse.

Whether or not some waters are "riggy", as we are often led to believe, I really do not know. Frankly, I doubt it. But if they are, they will only be those waters wherein the carp have already been caught too often—and I do not want to catch those anyway!

A rig, or terminal-tackle (call it what you will), needs to get a bait where we want it, be tangle-free, present the bait effectively, and hook and hold carp securely. Furthermore, it must do all this with minimum damage to the fish.

My general all-purpose, go-anywhere choice comprises an in-line Zipp lead, 15 in Nash fine, stiff anti-tangle tube, 15 lb test Merlin or The Edge hook-link (usually 15 in long), size six Mustad 34021 mounted line-aligner style (more about that presently), and a 2½ cm dental-floss hair. Invariably this is fished fixed-lead style, by means of a short length of silicon-tube pushed over the protruding peg on the lead and jammed over the barrel of the hook-link swivel (Figs 2 & 3). Oh, by the way, it must be proper silicon and not ordinary valve-rubber; silicon is very durable but valve-rubber will tear and split in use, and will require constant replacement. Good swivels are important too: Berkley, Drennan and Mustad are all reliable. Size 10 is the most useful.

If I am fishing in very dangerous circumstances, such as near snags, rocks or canal locks and piles, I use a 20 lb to 25 lb hook-link, and increase the hook-size to a size four, or really exceptionally, a size two. All other details remain the same.

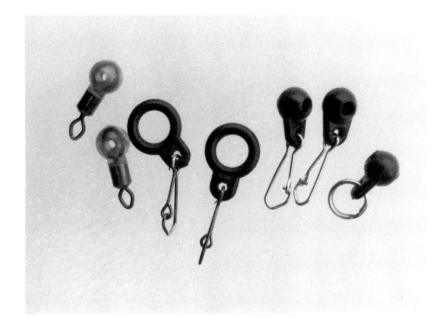

Rig-bits: Nash swivel-beads, Robert's free-run beads (with which I am experimenting), leger-beads equipped with clips and with split-ring.

For fishing at maximum range I prefer to use a lead mounted pendulum-style because it has better aerodynamic qualities. I generally use a John Roberts anti-tangle rig; it is fished fixed-lead style by joining the hook-link swivel and the rig's protruding end with a short length of silicon tube (Fig 4). The hook-link will be 14 lb Super-Silk or 15 lb Drennan Hi-Tenacity, because these are less prone to tangling with a pendulum-lead than are softer braids.

Many anglers cover the lead-link with tubing, believing that it reduces the likelihood of tangles. I have not found it to be so, so do not bother.

Alternatively I may use a bait-clip rig (Fig 5), which permits the use of any hook-link material, even floss, because tangles are impossible.

The curved protrusion below the lead provides the means by which the hook-link is tensioned and kept separate from the anti-tangle tube. This tensioned separation is what makes the rig 100 per cent tangle-free.

The bait is tied to the clip with PVA tape or thread, thus preventing the hook-link flailing round in flight and thereby making the terminal-tackle more aerodynamic. This improves both distance and accuracy.

I devised it for those occasions when I want to get every last yard out of my casting, but have since discovered that it has several unexpected

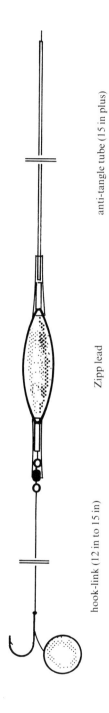

anti-tangle tube (15 in plus)

Zipp lead

hook-link (12 in to 15 in)

Fig. 2. In-line fixed-lead rig.

2 mm silicon-tube joining peg and anti-tangle tube

2 mm silicon-tube locking swivel and peg together

Fig. 3. In-line fixed-lead detail.

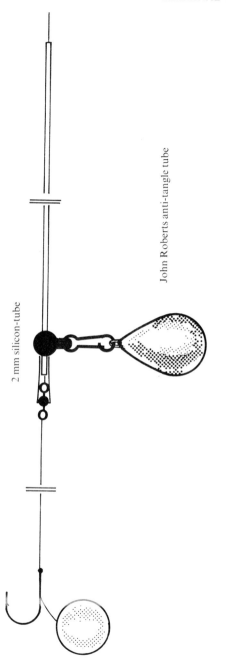

2 mm silicon-tube

John Roberts anti-tangle tube

Fig. 4. Pendulum-lead anti-tangle rig.

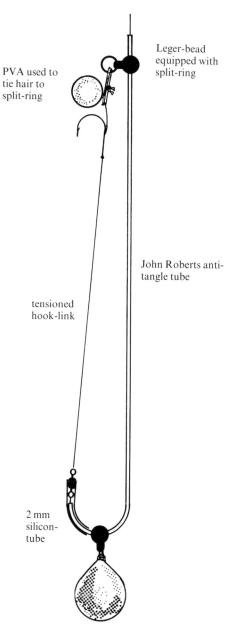

PVA used to
tie hair to
split-ring

Leger-bead
equipped with
split-ring

John Roberts anti-
tangle tube

tensioned
hook-link

2 mm
silicon-
tube

Fig. 5. Bait-clip rig.

Geordie Mike whiles away the time with a book (not *Big Water Carp*!). Coinciden-
tally, just minutes after this picture was taken . . . he turned the page!

extra advantages. It enables the rod to be lower at the commencement
of a cast (there being no hanging hook-link), thereby permitting a longer
power-stroke and, all being well, increased distance. It is also less likely
to catch on overhanging branches when casting from beneath a tree-
canopy; and it is easier to tuck between snags or lilies, whatever range
is being fished.

Those advantages became apparent because I actually use "my" rigs
before I write about them . . .!

I put "My" in inverted commas because when I showed this bait-clip
rig to Geordie Mike he said, "That's like E.T.'s tangle-free, long-cast
deadbait rig."

I had not seen Eddie Turner's version at the time but have since;
and Mike was right. But there are subtle differences that I believe make
mine better. I leave you to judge for yourself. Not that the principle
of the bait-clip is a new one anyway; beach anglers have used it for years.

Some anglers to whom I have shown it worry about the fact that
the bait will lay alongside the anti-tangle tube after the PVA has dissolved.
The tackle can be straightened by pulling back, of course, but most of
the waters I fish are too weedy or have too much bottom debris to make

this a practical or wise proposition; so I leave it exactly where it lands. The proximity of the bait and anti-tangle tube does not trouble me because I doubt that carp can distinguish between tubing, and normal lake-bottom clutter such as sticks, weed stalks etc. I only worry about tubing when I think it possible that waves or surface debris plucking at the line might cause it to move. But that problem, if indeed it is a problem, is easily solved by using a back-lead.

A terminal-tackle I use when I want to employ a longer than usual hook-link is what these days is generally called the "helicopter-rig" (Figs 6 & 7). The rig, however, goes back a lot further than the name, and evolved from a popular east coast cod-tackle. Rod Hutchinson described an adaptation in *The Carp Strikes Back*, he called it a silt rig; and in the second edition of *Modern Specimen Hunting* you can see my paternoster version of it.

I use it for delicate presentation of soft, "natural" baits (and a heavier version for fishing over weed, but that subject is dealt with at length in Chapter Ten). Worms are my favourite "natural", especially reds and gilt-tails. They are excellent and under-used carp bait but require relatively small hooks, fine line and a hook-link of approximately four feet. They should be hooked head-end only; forget any nonsense you may have read about hooking worms twice through the middle.

The circumstances under which light tackle can be used are obviously limited to waters that are virtually weed-free and snag-free; but where it is safe to do so, I use a hook-link of five pounds test (I prefer mono for this rig), and hooks no larger than size 10.

I caught a lot of carp on this set-up at Layer; and even tweaked one out of Yately Match Lake on the first and only occasion I fished there. This, it must be said, was to the considerable chagrin of a very well-known angler who was into the fifth day of what proved to be a week-long blank! Despite my success, I never went back because there were a lot of car-park thefts and break-ins at that time; and I cannot enjoy my fishing if I am worried that some retard will take my car, or leave me with the expense and inconvenience of a repair. There is a solution of course; as was discovered by Darenth regulars a few years back. Fed up with regular and frequent car-park vandalism, they lay in wait one night and, sure enough, a group of local youths appeared on the scene. The anglers intercepted them before they had a chance to do any damage, and explained very carefully, and with unambiguous clarity, the error of their ways. The anglers were obviously very persuasive because the youths never reappeared!

The only other rig I use to any extent, and in truth I do not use it very often, is Ken Townley's extending hook-link, usually in conjunction with a running lead. The hook-link is longer than usual, two feet is about right, and folded back on itself concertina-style. This is achieved by first

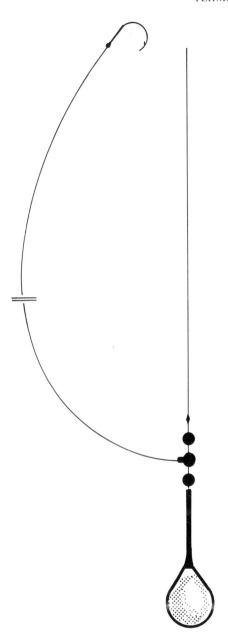

Fig. 6. Rotary (helicopter) rig.

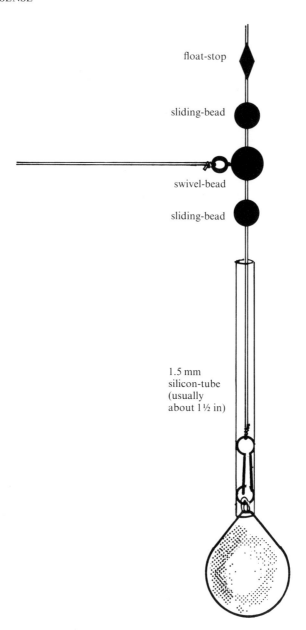

float-stop

sliding-bead

swivel-bead

sliding-bead

1.5 mm
silicon-tube
(usually
about 1½ in)

Fig. 7. Rotary-rig detail. NB. Do not tie the line direct to the lead, or breakages
will occur. Always tie it to a link of some sort.

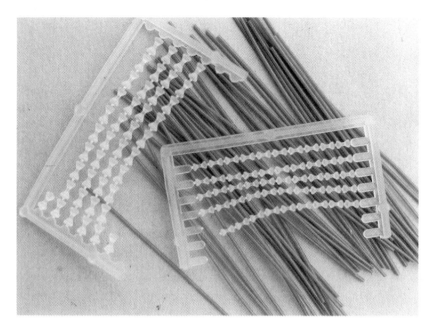

Drennan boilie-stops, I like these. Also shown are nylon bristles from a yard-broom, boilie-stops that cost about £2 for a lifetime's supply!

coating it with Kryston's Super-Stiff anti-tangle gel, whereupon it will stick to itself readily. I then bind the top and bottom of the concertina section with a short length of PVA tape to hold everything secure for casting (Fig 8).

The first time I used this rig was on an occasion when I was getting lots of twitches and rod-top knocks, but no runs on my standard in-line fixed-lead. The change to the concertina-rig certainly produced runs, but they were all from tench and bream! Still, it proved that the rig worked.

I cannot honestly recall an occasion when I have been compelled to use the concertina-rig in order to get strikeable takes from carp; but there have been several occasions when I have chosen to use it and caught carp by so doing.

In truth, most times standard, efficient, tangle-free rigs, tied with reliable components, put carp on the bank. Which is not to say that they should be used slavishly and without thought; occasionally a little bit of fine-tuning may be necessary. If fish are missed on the strike, it **could** be that the hair is too long and they are not taking the hook fully into their mouth. If carp are dropped while being played, it **might** be

Footnote: I now use the concertina-rig a lot, even with my standard fixed-lead tackles. It has proved very successful.

I do a lot of my rig-tying while fishing.

that the hook-link is too short and not giving the fish adequate opportunity to take the bait confidently. If carp are eating all the "freebies" but not taking the hook-bait, it **could** be that the hair is too short and the carp are having their suspicions aroused by the hook-bait behaving differently to free-offerings.

On the other hand—missed runs might not be runs at all, they might be line-bites. Dropped fish might simply be due to not striking properly. And as for those carp that are eating all the "freebies"—how do you know? Divers who went down in one of my local pits told me that there were thousands upon thousands of rotting boilies on the bottom; and a netting operation on a lake near Hastings produced no carp but **did** dredge up half a tonne of boilies!

So it could be that the carp are eating neither the hook-baits **nor** the freebies!

Sometimes I cannot help being reminded of the Great Computer in Hitch-Hiker's Guide To The Galaxy. After taking untold millions of years coming up with the answer "42", in response to having been instructed to find the Meaning of Life, the Universe and Everything; told the puzzled recipients of the information to "Go away and find the question."

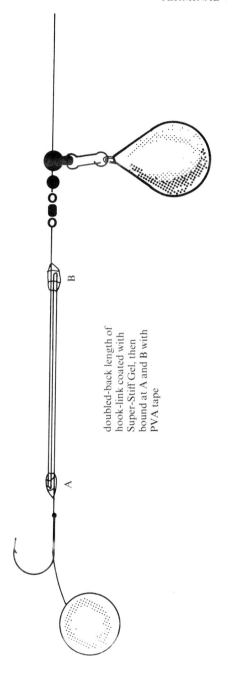

doubled-back length of
hook-link coated with
Super-Stiff Gel, then
bound at A and B with
PVA tape

Fig. 8. Concertina-rig.

This angler has solved the increasing problem of car-park vandalism . . . but I favour the Darenth Solution.

In other words—we need to identify the problem before we can find a solution; indeed, we need to ensure that we **have** a problem. But whether the problem is real or imagined; we will not solve it by haphazardly blundering about and introducing random elements that may only serve to exacerbate matters. Here is an example—two or three fish drop off—we panic. A hook pattern on which we have successfully landed scores of fish is rejected and new ones tried. We try larger sizes, then smaller. Maybe the fixed-lead is the culprit? We try it running. The hook-link is shortened, then lengthened . . . and what about the hair length . . .?

Does that sequence of events have a familiar ring about it? We have all "been there", as they say; and 99 per cent of the time have failed to find the answer. We may even have made the situation worse. Had we stuck with the proven system the problem might well have disappeared of its own accord, having been just "one of those things". I am not advocating unthinking acceptance of failure; if problems occur, of course we should try to find solutions—but what I am cautioning against are random, panic-responses to unidentified difficulties that may not even exist.

There is, however, a problem that undoubtedly exists, but it is one

Gardner rig-bin for hook-link storage. By joining the hook of one link to the swivel
of the next, scores of links can be stored.

that most of the time we are not even aware of. And that is the simple
fact that a number of carp pick up the bait and given no registration
at all. My friend Ken Crow had a dramatic demonstration of this when
he decided to test some rigs on a group of carp to which he was giving
a temporary home in a holding-pool. He subsequently described to me
how those carp picked up the bait and backed off to the full length of
the hook-link then, with the bait still being held, moved round in an
arc before finally spitting it out. Ken said that the bait was often held
for several seconds, yet there had been no movement of his indicator.

Now I am not sure how much of a real problem this sort of thing
is in actual fishing situations. After all a carp might pick up a bait, reject
it and swim off; only to return and subsequently pick it up in a manner
that **does** result in a strikeable registration. So a proportion of missed
opportunities might end up not being missed at all. But I think it fair
to assume that we certainly miss some. A few anglers, as I said before,
respond to this by making their alarms ultra-sensitive; but frankly I cannot
see the point of this. If I am laying back on my bed-chair, I am unable
to respond to an isolated "bleep" emitted by an alarm that has been

finely sensitised. Is anyone? I think this is one of those things that impresses readers, but has little application to real fishing situations!

Although I am philosophical about the fact that I undoubtedly lose a certain number of opportunities, I try not to get too complacent about the inevitability of the wastage.

One way of dealing with ultra-sensitive takes in certain circumstances is to use a float. I am not qualified to give information on float-fishing techniques because, frankly, I am not a very good float angler. The best advice I can give is that you read articles and books by successful match-anglers on the subject. There was some really good material produced in the days before they all went pole-made, and if you are interested it is worth your while browsing the shelves of your local library. The following references will repay some study:

The Match Fisherman, edited by David Hall; Chapter 7, "Shotting Patterns" by Max Winters

World Class Match Fishing by Kevin Ashurst with Colin Dyson; Chapter 6, "Stillwater Floats"

Match Angling edited by the late John Carding; Chapter 5, "Long-Range Float-Fishing in Still and Slow Water" by Dave Rossi.

The last named is a paper-back that was published nearly 20 years ago but in its yellowing pages lies some of the best advice ever on bait-preparation and groundbaiting.

I especially recommend that you try to get hold of another book from the same era: *Ivan Marks on Match Fishing* by Ivan Marks and John Goodwin. Again it is a paperback and when published sold for the princely sum of 85p! I picked up my copy from a remainders-stall in a local bookshop for an exorbitant 25p! I can state unreservedly that this little publication is one of the most useful books I own. I am a bit of a philistine with books and tend to give them away; I recently gave a boxful to a friend who, being a collector, would value them more than I would. I did not sell them, I gave them away. But Ivan's paperback is one I would never part with; single-handedly it did more to change my approach to light-line leger methods than anything else I had ever read. So do not be put off by the fact that the book was published in 1975 because, contrary to what some younger readers might imagine, specialist angling has been around for a long, long while. If you want to learn about float-fishing, ultra-sensitive legering and "natural" baits like maggots and casters, this book is without equal.

Occasionally the standard bottom-fishing set-ups are modified slightly to accommodate different circumstances—the most obvious of which is the use of pop-ups. These are currently very popular and many anglers use them almost exclusively. I use them comparatively little. But when I do want to use an anchored pop-up I use either putty-weight round a rubber float-stop (Fig 9), or a shot pinched over a small piece

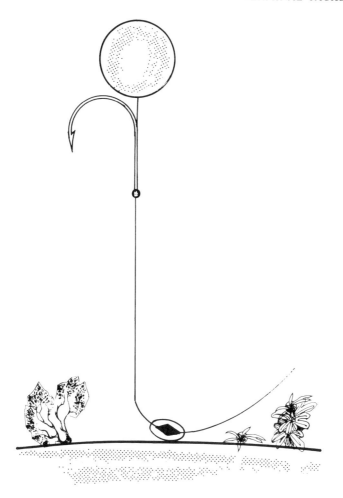

Fig. 9. Pop-up anchored with putty-weight.

of 0.5 mm rig-tube (Fig 10). I prefer the shot for long-range fishing due to its extra security, and when I am using fairly large or buoyant pop-ups. The subtlety of the putty-weight is ideal for critical-balancing because it lends itself to adjustment.

For several seasons, due largely to Rob Maylin's writings, critically-balanced pop-ups were very in-vogue; then Bruce Ashby wrote a piece in *Carp Fisher* number 20 (summer 1991) in which he described how

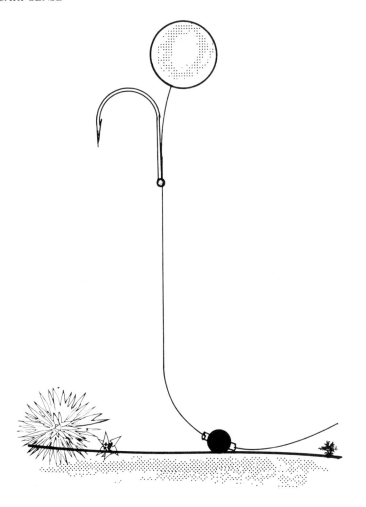

Fig. 10. Pop-up anchored with shot.

he watched such baits wafting up from the bottom due to water movement created by feeding carp, which often resulted in them not being taken. Heavily weighted pop-ups, by contrast, remained anchored and were taken readily. He concluded that not only was it unnecessary to critically balance, but could be a distinct disadvantage.

As I have already said, I do not use pop-ups very often, but find them effective in winter and useful for fishing above silt or silkweed (Fig

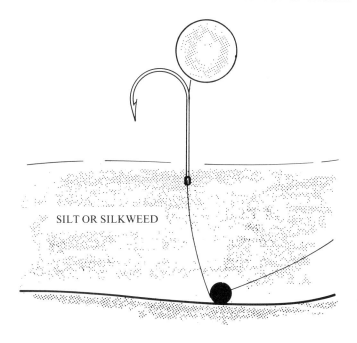

SILT OR SILKWEED

Fig. 11. Pop-up over silt or silkweed.

11). Very buoyant pop-ups have another advantage that I have never seen mentioned; they resist being buried by bream. Kevin Gardner pointed this out to me, having used it to mitigate a bream problem in a big French barrage. That was before he quit the mists of fenland to go and live in sunny Queensland, down in "Oz"'.

When I use pop-ups, I usually use them in conjunction with a sinker on the same hair (Fig 12). I call this sit-up-and-beg presentation, but recently I saw it described as looking like a little snowman. It does too! And what a lovely description.

Alternatively I use a little piece of rig-foam sandwiched between a couple of boilie cubes. If the top cube is smaller than the lower one, the baits sit up on the bottom nice and neatly (Fig 13). This achieves three purposes, any one of which might be the reason for using the arrangement. It produces a bait that will rest lightly on silt or bottom silkweed, thus remaining in view; it keeps the top bait clear of silt so it does not become contaminated by that horrible "ooze" smell; and it achieves a critically balanced bait, for those occasions when such a presentation is deemed necessary.

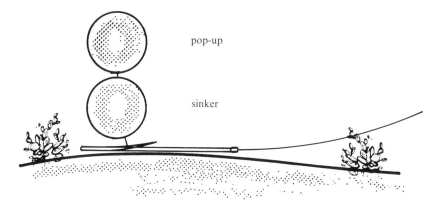

Fig. 12. Sit-up-and-beg "snowman" presentation.

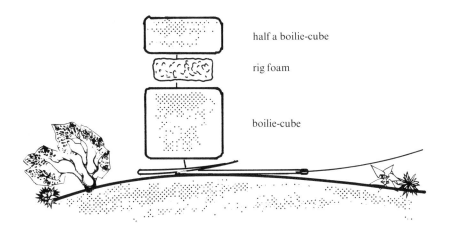

Fig. 13. Critically-balanced boilie-cubes. (The rig-foam is trimmed until critical-balancing is achieved.

THE LINE-ALIGNER

Following the introduction of my line-aligner (Fig 14) in *Carpworld* number eight (June/July 1990), quite a lot of anglers have told me that they were unable to tie it—but on being shown how to do it have conceded that whilst it is undoubtedly a bit fiddly, it is not actually that difficult.

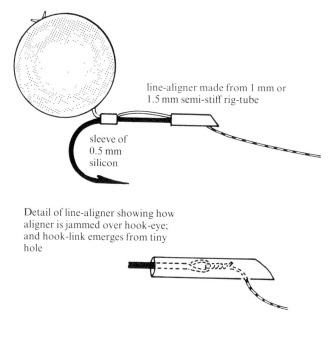

line-aligner made from 1 mm or
1.5 mm semi-stiff rig-tube

sleeve of
0.5 mm
silicon

Detail of line-aligner showing how
aligner is jammed over hook-eye;
and hook-link emerges from tiny
hole

Fig. 14. The line-aligner.

I therefore wrote a follow-up piece in *Carpworld* number 15 (July 1991) in which I described the procedure stage by stage.

For the benefit of those who did not see the second feature, I shall repeat the assembly instructions here. The combination of words and pictures should make everything clear.

1. Tie on the hook—in the photograph I have used a size six Mustad 34021 and 15 lb braid. Push a sewing needle into a 15 mm length of 1 mm or 1.5 mm diameter stiff rig-tube; the larger diameter tube is easier to work with, but produces a slightly bulkier aligner.

Instead of passing the needle right through the tube, bring it out of the side about two thirds of the way along. Thread the braid through the eye of the needle.

2. Push the length of rig-tube off the needle and down the hook-link.

3. Pass the needle, blunt end first, through the rig-tube, and pass the tag-end of the hook knot through the needle-eye.

4. Pull the tag-end through the rig-tube by withdrawing the needle.

5. Touch the knot with a tiny dab of Superglue—do not use too much

or the glue will run along the hook-link and make it go stiff, which rather defeats the object of using an ultra-soft hook-link material.

6. Tie the hair in position—my choice, as you can see from the photograph, is for a floss hair tied to the eye of the hook (and secured with Superglue) with its pivot-point set by means of a short length of rig-tube.

7. Now for the only difficult bit of the whole procedure—the rig-tube must be pushed down over the eye of the hook. It may not sound like a difficult operation but you will find in practice that 1.0 mm tube especially is most reluctant to pass over the combined bulk of the knot and the hook-eye.

8. When the rig-tube is correctly positioned, that is with the hook-link emerging from the tube on the **inside** of the shank (the side facing the hook-point), I trim the tube to a 30 degree angle. The surplus tag-end is trimmed at the same time.

9. The swivel is tied-on and the knot touched with a dab of glue—but this time I use 1.5 mm soft rig-tube to finish off, it being very much easier to handle than is the rigid variety.

10. The final photograph shows the completed hook-link.

I concede that the line-aligner set-up does not look particularly neat—although it looks neater in use than it does in photographs—but there is no questioning its efficiency and effectiveness. I have been using it for more than two seasons now and have found that with the exception of one particularly frustrating week's fishing in France, it has given very secure hook-holds. If we discount the French week, and I have to admit that I am not **completely** sure that it is legitimate to do so, I have only had one drop-off and, unlikely though it may seem, no missed runs at all.

THAT FRENCH WEEK?

That was frustrating in the extreme; brother Rick, our French hosts, Michel and Philippe Mahin, and I, suffered a succession of thrown hooks as big, powerful fish ploughed slowly up and down the margins during the final stages of some of the most protracted fights I have ever experienced. Three of my losses were particularly painful as they were 30 lb-class fish. One was a mid/upper thirty that was hooked at the tail-end of the day, and was still being played 40 minutes later when darkness fell. Rick, Michel and Philippe, all of whom had packed up by then, sat on the grassy bank behind me and watched. Occasionally I heard quiet murmurings from them; but most of the time they just sat and shared my anxiety. A lot of fish over the preceding few days had come adrift, and we knew this was a very big one, so the tension inhibited conversation.

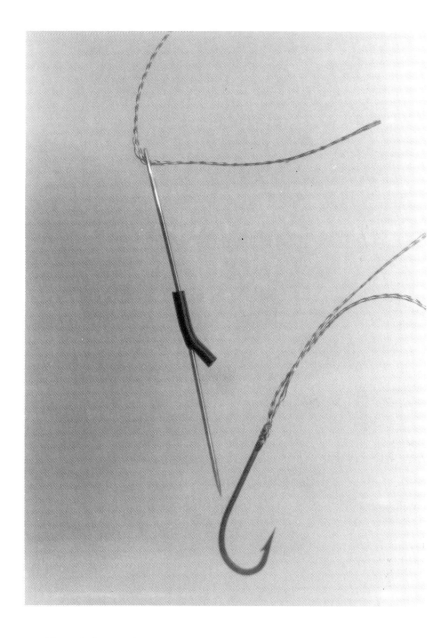

Tie on the hook and push needle in rig-tube ensuring that it emerges from the side.

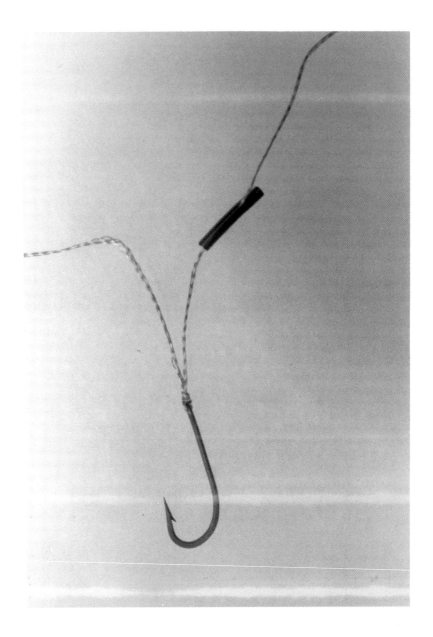

Push rig-tube off needle and down hook-link.

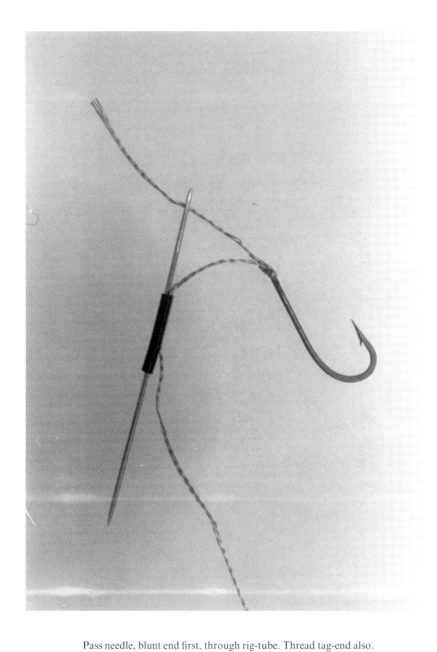

Pass needle, blunt end first, through rig-tube. Thread tag-end also.

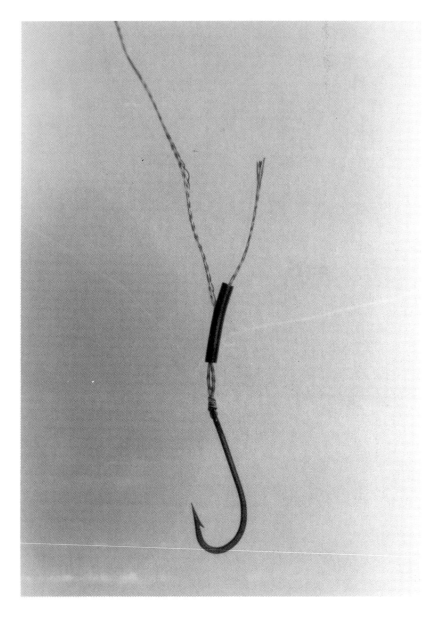

Pull tag-end through rig-tube.

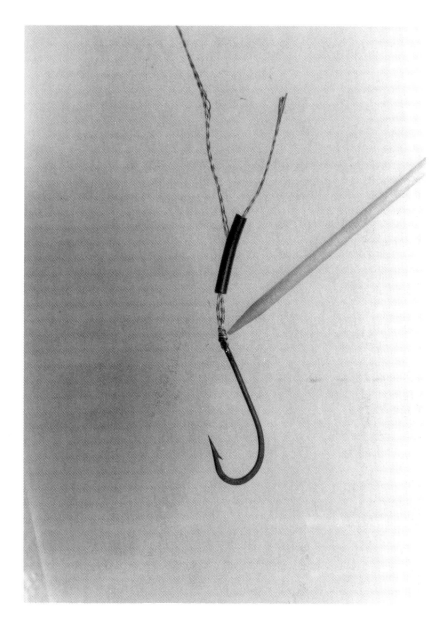

Touch knot with Superglue.

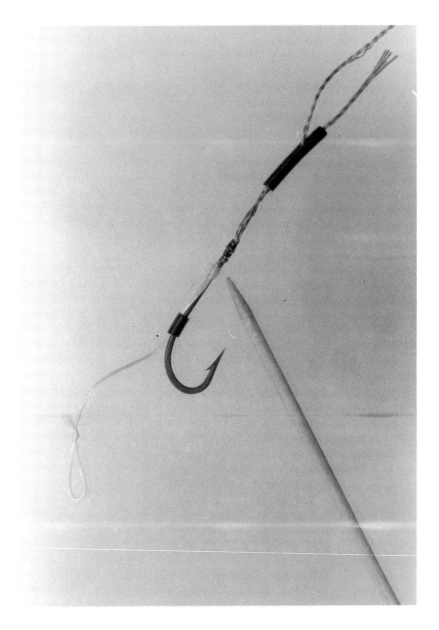

Tie hair—I have used floss.

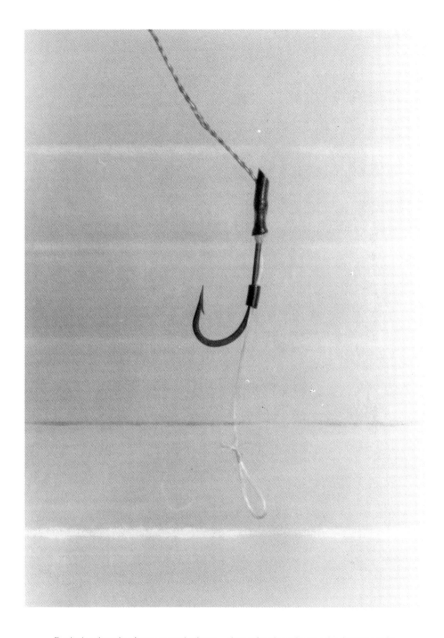

Push the rig-tube down over the knot—then trim the tube at a 30 degree angle.

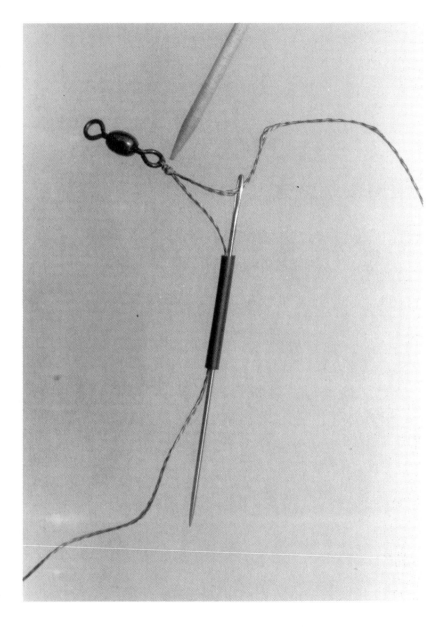

Tie on swivel—secure knot with Superglue.

Mike nets a fish for French Pierre.

Sunny winter weather on a big south coast pit. I caught three that day.

They don't have to be big. This March 15 pounder came from a difficult water
and made my pulse race.

They didn't all drop off – this is my $31\frac{1}{4}$ common from the "Lake of Tears". Thank you Michel!

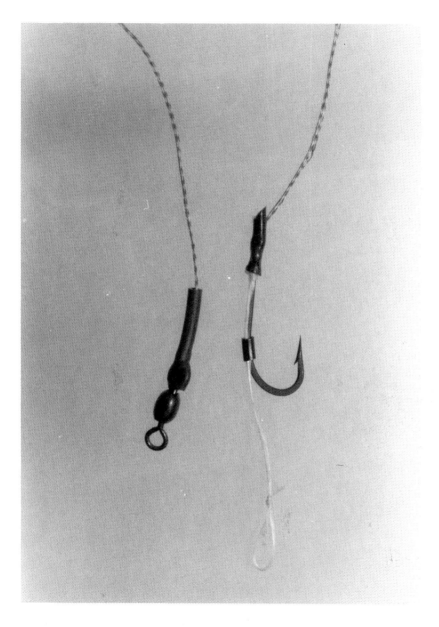

The completed hook-link.

Eventually; predictably and inevitably, the hook pulled.

I turned to my companions, shrugged with despair, and disconsolately dismantled my rod. I was so distressed that I could not talk—I was too deflated and disappointed even to curse. I could have just sat down and cried.

We tried everything we could think of, but to no avail. God, it was exasperating! Rick thought he might have solved the problem when he dug out some long forgotten Shakespeare hooks from his tackle-box. He had used them with success many years before to deal with an almost identical situation. The hooks had a round bend, and on discussing it afterwards we wondered if that fact had been significant. We thought it could be the best shape for coping with the constantly changing direction of pull during a long fight. This was pure speculation on our part, and we did not get the chance to firm-up on the theory because the holiday ended; and when we returned home, all was well with the world and fish stayed hooked!

Michel subsequently wrote to me and said he had solved the difficulty by using Drennan Starpoints. Whether or not they would have kept us connected to fish on that particular trip is impossible to say; but if they had, I would have acquired at least three more thirties to my credit! I look forward to a return trip to put them to the test.

I managed one thirty-plus though—but only just. It was on our last day, and the heat was so oppressive that I drank bottle after bottle of water to keep from dehydration. Then in the middle of the afternoon, when the heat was practically unbearable, I had a run! It was obvious from the outset that it was a big fish; but in a strange way I was not concerned because I was waiting for that sickening but inevitable moment when the hook would drop out! But as the fight progressed, and the fish remained attached, I started to hope that maybe, just maybe, I might land it. That was when my mouth went dry with panic!

Eventually it came within clear viewing range, and it was apparent that it was not merely big, but very big. We could see it was a common too. Michel picked up the net and crouched quietly at the water's edge. He looked very calm and confident. I found that reassuring!

After a number of last-minute surges, every one of which shortened my life I am certain, I drew it towards the waiting net. Suddenly it was in! I have never seen smoother or slicker netting in my life—mind you, those French lads get plenty of practice!

I reached down into the meshes to unhook the fish whilst it was still in the water—and found that the hook had dropped out! I strongly suspect that had the netsman been anyone other than Michel, it would have been another lost thirty.

Thank you Michel—netsman par excellence!

So except in Le Lac des Larmes (The Lake of Tears—not its real

One of the compensations of a frustrating French week, civilised lunchtimes! Alain, Rick and Michel savour the shade. All baits were retrieved, incidentally!

name, but appropriate under the circumstances), I am completely happy with the line-aligner. It works because it encourages the hook to turn and snag on a carp's lower lip, no matter which way the hook happens to be facing. In his book *Fox Pool*, Rob Maylin described this in relation to the bent-hook and explained how it could be tested using Clive Williams' finger snagging test.

The turning effect with both the bent-hook and the line-aligner depends on a very soft hook-link being used; and for that reason it works better with 15 lb braid than with 20 lb. It does not work at all with a mono hook line.

In the case of the bent-hook, the turning moment is achieved because the point of hook-link attachment is inside the line of the shank. The same effect occurs with the line-aligner not because of the attachment point, but because the link emerges from the inside of the shank. This duplicates what happens with spade-end patterns; which was what led me to devise the line-aligner in the first place. It was not, however, the first idea that came to mind. Initially I tried to produce an inturned eye by bending it with pliers; but the carbon steel from which Mustad's 34021 was made would not withstand that sort of abuse. There are a lot of

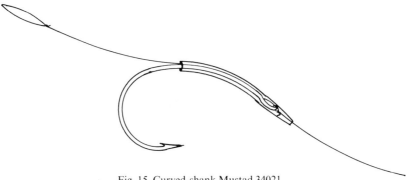

Fig. 15. Curved-shank Mustad 34021.

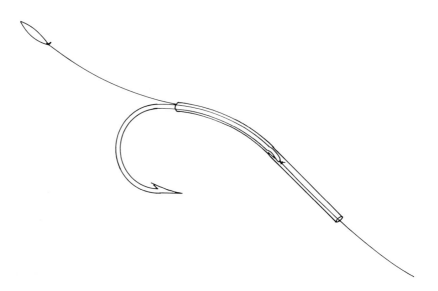

Fig. 16. Curved-shank 34021 extended with semi-rigid rig-tube.

down-eyed production hooks on the market, of course, but none I considered wholly suitable for carp fishing.

Next I tried putting a curve in the shank so it was a bit like the hooks on which fly-tiers tie shrimp patterns (Fig 15). This modification was quite successful and I caught a number of fish on it.

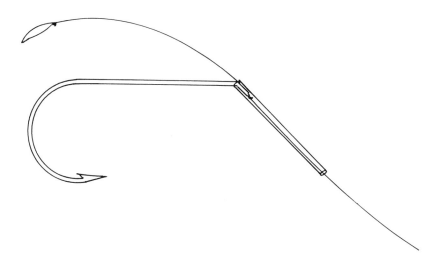

Fig. 17. Richard Donnelly's version of the bent-hook; achieved by jamming semi-rigid
rig-tube over the eye of a down-eyed hook.

The next idea was to extend the curved shank with a length of semi-rigid plastic rig-tube (Fig 16). This worked too, and was similar to the idea independently thought-up by Richard Donnelly (Fig 17) and published in the now defunct CAA's autumn '90 magazine *Carp Catcher*. Proof that when faced with the same problem, anglers' minds will often converge.

Richard claims, incidentally, that the rig-tube version of the bent-hook retains the efficiency of the pattern, but does not damage fish the way the bent-hook allegedly does. I have no opinions on the efficiency of the bent-hook, nor its tendency to damage or stitch-up mouths because I have never used it. Frankly, I think what damages carp more than anything is repeated capture, irrespective of what pattern of hook is used. In hard-fished waters like Bysingwood, Layer and Horton Kirby, we used to catch carp with damaged mouths years ago, long before the bent-hook had been thought of. Possibly the bent-hook exacerbates the problem; I am not qualified to comment. But the only way we can ensure that tissue damage is limited and gets a chance to properly heal, is to drastically restrict fishing on pressured waters. And I cannot see that being a very realistic prospect.

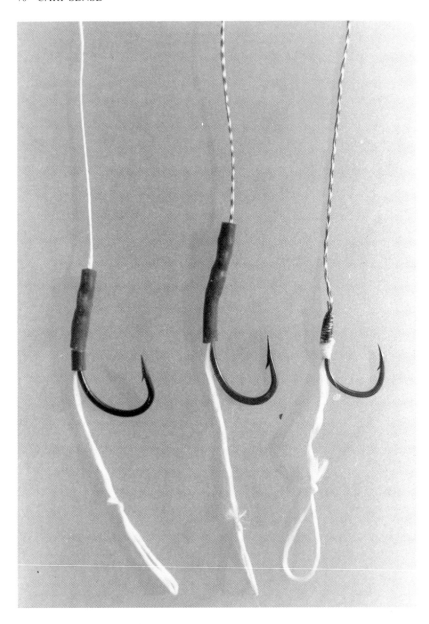

Shrimp-back bend in an experimental pattern (which I no longer use), and a Mustad 34021. On the right is one of my favourites, the Owner spade-end.

LEADS

Recently there has been a lot of discussion about the use of very heavy leads. I have just glanced at an advertisement and seen round-leads up to six ounces listed.

I do not honestly know where I stand on this one. I remember that initially the use of two ounce leads seemed crude because we had been conditioned to use as little lead as possible; but I adapted to the change and was soon using two ounce leads as a matter of course, and three to four ounce versions for long-range fishing. So is there anything inherently wrong with using five and six ounce leads? And if not; where does it end? If six ounce leads are okay; why not half a pound?

As I said, I do not quite know where I stand on this one; but my instincts tell me that it is going too far. I do not doubt the efficiency of very heavy leads, and I have no doubt that if I used heavier leads I would certainly hook some of the drop-backs that I currently miss. But heavy leads require heavy rods; and if they are to be cast any significant distance demand the use of a **very** heavy shock-leader to prevent snap-offs when casting. I cannot imagine that I would enjoy using either the brutish rods or the very heavy leaders; so I shall stick with my existing rods and use leads to a maximum of four ounces.

There is, however, a not commonly realised fact that can give the advantage of a heavy lead without actually having to use one. A lead mounted pendulum-style tends to bed-in the bottom more than does an in-line lead. The extent to which this happens depends on the depth of water and the nature of the bottom. It can take quite a tug to free it which, in turn, results in a two or three ounce lead having the characteristics of a much heavier one at the critical moment when a carp pulls the hook-link tight and the hook snags against its lip.

In-line leads land horizontally, which makes bedding-in much less likely.

Does it make much difference? I do not think so, which is why I am happy to use in-line leads most of the time.

Pursuing the point; how much of what we do in terms of rig development really matters? To what extent do we catch carp **because** of our choice of hook-link material, hook pattern, hook size, tail-length, weight of lead etc; and to what extent do we catch carp **despite** our choices? I do not know the answer to that one; but when I find myself getting bogged down by minutiae, I often recall the late Oliver Kite's lovely comment regarding lure fishing for trout, "You chuck it out; pull it back; and when you can't, you've got one."

Only a fool would claim that Oliver Kite's tongue-in-cheek disdainful denial of subtlety in trout fishing is true; and I would be the last to suggest that it is applicable to carp fishing. But what **is** true is that we sometimes make carp fishing far more complicated than it need be, and in so doing make the job of catching them more difficult than it really is.

First, as the man said, we must find our fish. Having done so; we must present a good bait on an efficient rig, and if they are willing to feed at all, we will catch them.

Carp are not clever; they do not have to be outwitted. By fishing for them and catching them we do, however, teach them to be cautious and suspicious. We merely have to overcome that caution and suspicion; and complicated rigs are not the means by which that is best achieved.

Which brings me back to the comment with which I started this chapter; namely that most successful carp anglers actually use a very limited repertoire of rigs; and they are standard ones, believe me—no matter what they write in their articles!

3 Boilie Discourse

I am increasingly of the opinion that a great deal of the received wisdom on the subject of bait is misleading, and much of it, including a lot of what I hitherto believed myself, is incorrect. Trouble is, the subject has become embroiled in "science", which has led to many anglers being unnecessarily impressed and intimidated by those who use scientific language to back up their assertions.

I do not intend, however, embarking on an orgy of debunking, because scientific information can, or at least ought to be, helpful; but I think it is true to say that an awful lot of bait-writing falls into the category of the partially-sighted leading the blind! Hopefully I shall avoid doing that, and will try to express my beliefs and observations in a straightforward and commonsense manner.

FLAVOURS

Probably all solvent-based flavours, essential oils, bulk oils and oil-based flavours will function as labels to identify a bait that is used for prebaiting; but to see them **solely** as labels is to seriously underestimate their importance.

Many flavours appear to be inherently attractive to carp, but they are not equally so, and some are undoubtedly far more attractive than others. If you read bait suppliers' catalogues you will get the impression that all their flavours and oils are highly attractive and will produce runs on days when others do not etc. To an extent this is true in that a flavour of only moderate attraction used in a spot where carp are feeding, will undoubtedly out-perform a better flavour used in a swim devoid of fish! Such a fact should be obvious but tends not to be mentioned in product-catalogues! There are innumerable other variables that need to be considered too, among them being differences in angling ability, base-mix composition, time spent on the bank etc. I have read articles that seem to suggest that pH contrasts between flavours and the surrounding water or the bottom, may have a marked effect on their detectability or their attraction qualities; I have read too that some flavours may stand out better than others from ambient environmental chemical signals, and thus be more likely to be located. All of which may or may not be true, I am damned if I know! What I **do** know is that a good flavour is a good flavour is a good flavour . . . and works everywhere.

There is no possible way I or anyone else could subject the wide range of flavours currently available to objective comparison. It is in my nature to experiment, but I am also a pragmatist so tend to stick with one of the very small repertoire of flavours in which I have most confidence.

Among my favourites are: Scopex (Hutchinson and SBS), Strawberry Jam EA (SBS), Maplecreme and Ultraspice (Hutchinson), Golden Syrup and Pink Zing (Geoff Kemp), and Condensed Milk powder flavour (Colne Valley). I also like Colne Valley's Seafood Essence, but that is a natural extract and not a flavour. There are doubtless numerous others that work equally well, but you will have to rely on bankside recommendations or your own personal evaluation to find them.

I am not convinced that there are inherent advantages in one solvent-base over another. My favourites include flavours on iso propyl alcohol, propylene glycol, diacetin and ethyl alcohol. We frequently hear and read about particular solvent-bases "blowing" when a lot of carp are caught on them. Frankly I doubt it. I go further and say that I am not convinced that carp can readily detect them. Scientific evidence appears to support that suspicion, with regard to ethyl alcohol anyway (Reactions of Aquarium Carp to Food and Flavours, Howard A Loeb, New York Fish and Game Journal, Vol 7, No 1, January 1960).

The same paper, incidentally, records that no positive feeding reaction was evoked by any of the large number of oils (both bulk and essential) that were tested, with the exception of olive oil and soya oil containing sardine particles. Without the sardine particles they joined all the other oils in evoking no feeding reaction and producing indifference after tasting. Angling experience would appear to contradict those observations. Some of the essential-oils such as geranium, black pepper, ylang ylang, garlic and juniper berry have a lot of devotees, and their undoubted success is difficult to reconcile with Loeb's findings. One could argue that they are merely acting as labels, but their apparent effectiveness suggests that there is more to it than that. I do not have strong opinions on this because I am not a great fan of essential oils, but I am puzzled by the contradictions. I have fewer problems with bulk-oils such as are recommended by Premier Baits because they are not being used as attractors in isolation, they are used with fish-meals and therefore form part of a whole, and there is no denying the attraction of the resulting combination.

Recommended levels for flavours are given in all the bait-dealers' product catalogues, but my advice would be to regard these purely as starting points and conduct your own experiments. Actually I rarely include solvent-based flavour **in** my bait at all, preferring to spray it on boilies before freezing. As a guide, if the recommended flavour-level per one pound (454 g) dry-mix is 5 ml; I use half the amount (2.5 ml) with one pound of made-up boilies. When the lightly coated baits are taken out of the freezer and allowed to thaw prior to use, the flavour is drawn into the millimetre or so of outer skin. I believe that this aids detection and provides attraction, but does not significantly alter the taste of the bait. The actual taste of my bait is controlled by other ingredients and additives which I shall discuss presently.

Those who worry that sprayed flavour will only retain its attractiveness for a short time, might consider that when flavour is used in the usual way and incorporated in the mix, it leaches out from the skin of the bait readily enough but is extremely slow to leach out from the centre. The extent to which this locked-in flavour is detectable by carp is probably minimal. I prefer, therefore, to regard smell and taste as two separate entities. I realise that there must inevitably be overlap and a carp's chemo-reception system embodies both smell and taste receptors; but I am defining "smell" as that which is detectable via water-borne molecules; and taste as that which occurs when a bait is taken within the lips and mouth, thus making direct contact with the taste-buds, the more so when it is crushed by the pharyngeals.

In simple terms, therefore, I strive to produce baits that are readily detectable by means of a highly attractive "smell" comprising my chosen flavour and water soluble ingredients within the mix. I then want those baits to taste good, which I hope will encourage carp to actively search for more.

BASE MIXES

First there was the word; and the word was Wilton!

No discussion on modern carp baits can occur without Fred Wilton's name cropping up. His theory has been well documented, so I shall merely summarise by saying that the basis of his philosophy was that if a good quality, nutritious bait was introduced in sufficient quantity it would become an integral and possibly preferred part of a carp's diet. After experiments with dried meat and similar products, Fred eventually settled for a bait that consisted largely of refined milk proteins such as casein, lactalbumin and caseinates. These High-Protein (HP) or, as Fred preferred to call them, High Nutritional Value (HNV) baits, quickly became accepted as the baits by which all others were judged. Protein level and the digestibility of same became something of a Holy Grail, and hardcore baitmen strived for higher and higher protein levels; they also added enzymes in the hope that the convertibility of the protein within their baits would be improved. Baits containing high levels of cereal-derived products such as soya flour, semolina or maize flour were denigratingly referred to as "crap baits" or, at best, "carrier baits", implying that they were okay for carrying attractive flavours and the like, but were otherwise very poor substitutes suitable only for one-off quickie-sessions.

We were wrong.

Our main mistake was in our all-year use of refined milk products as the major component. I have spent a small fortune over the years on casein etc., because like so many others I was seduced by the knowledge that carp were efficient converters of milk proteins, and I was further seduced by the idea that water soluble milk products such as caseinates might evoke chemically induced nutritional-recognition. It was a neat theory, and intellectually satisfying.

Unfortunately carp did not play ball. To start with they demonstrated an illogical liking for many beans, pulses and nuts. Nuts in general, and tiger-nuts in particular, were especially problematical to committed milk-protein fans because they seemed to pass virtually unchanged through the carp's digestive tract. It was evident that carp were getting very little nutritional benefit from tiger-nuts, but they kept eating them.

Various explanations were put forward to explain this aberration in carp behaviour, including the anthropomorphic "Well, we smoke tobacco even though it's harmful."

The defence of milk-proteins became even more desperate when carp in all manner of waters demonstrated not merely a willingness to take so called "crap baits" such as Richworth ready-mades, but seemed to exhibit a marked preference for them! Baffled milk-protein fans listened to the deafening silence of their Optonics while users of Tutti-Fruttis and Tropicanos caught carp! This turn of events severely tested the ingenuity and creativity of milk-protein users, but they proved equal to the task and found the answer—availability. The paradox was explained; ready-mades were inferior baits, but were proving more successful due to mass use. Nice one! Except that not so long ago I seem to recall that those same milk-protein enthusiasts were arguing that the angler who used something different to everyone else, and thus exploited a nutritional niche, would clean up. Come on . . . they can't have it both ways!

I did not accept that theory, but did consider it likely that users of "poor quality" ready-mades were benefiting from groundbaiting done with HNV baits—in other words, carp had become conditioned to eating little round balls, and all the time they were in nutritional-profit by so doing, would continue to do so. That explanation **might** have explained acceptance, but certainly did **not** explain preference!

HNV milk-protein boilies; I now believe the basic theory to have been wrong.

So why do carp so frequently demonstrate a preference for what are perceived to be nutritionally inferior baits? I have come to the conclusion that it is not a paradox at all, the question being based on an assumption that does not withstand scrutiny. Who says that ready-mades and other cereal-based baits are nutritionally inferior? Milk-protein fans might be interested to learn that scientists involved in aquaculture have found that excessive amounts of protein in relation to non-protein energy sources, suppress both growth rate and appetite.

Those same scientists and aquaculturists have also found that a 32 per cent protein diet appears to be optimum, assuming that energy requirements are also adequately met. (*Nutrition and Feeding of Fish*, Tom Lovell, Van Nostrand Reinhold, New York). A far cry from 80 per cent milk-protein HNV's, with or without supposed enzyme enhancement!

And what sort of recipe would produce a 32 per cent protein bait? Well, a 50/50 soya/semolina mix bound with eggs would come pretty close ... how strange that such a recipe is almost identical to many so-called "crap baits"! Seems they might be nutritionally sound after all.

The success of cereal-based baits could also be due in part to the not altogether improbable explanation that carp might like the taste of them!

There is something else that could be relevant to the discussion. I wrote about this in an article entitled "Protein Level—The Missing Link?" (*Carpworld* March/April 1990), when I suggested a possible correlation between protein level and water temperature, and said that this might explain the apparent superiority of particles and cereal-based baits over milk-protein baits in summer and autumn. In winter, on the other hand, I wrote that I have found milk protein baits to be superior.

It is evident that it is not purely a protein thing though, because boilies based on fish-meals are highly effective in summer and autumn, yet they qualify for the HP or HNV designation.

So obviously it is not solely a protein/temperature correlation, as I had incorrectly supposed it to be in my *Carpworld* article. For a while I thought the likelihood that milk-proteins would rapidly sour in warm water was the key to their reduced effectiveness in summer and autumn. I still believe that to be a significant factor, but I had an experience that made me wonder if there might be more to it, and the attractiveness or otherwise of milk-proteins might in some way be directly linked with water temperature, quite independently of bacterial activity.

It occurred when brother Martin and I were fishing a local pit on a fairly regular basis through autumn and early winter. It was not a difficult water and one or the other, or both of us, caught a fish most trips. We each used nuts on one rod and HNV cubes with a high milk-protein content on the other rod. Free-bait amounts were identical, comprising two or three pouches round each hook-bait. What I found so fascinating was that when we fished during a cold-snap, or after an early morning frost, or in a bitingly cold wind, our fish without exception fell to HNV cubes. During mild spells all fish bar one fell to nuts. The fact that we caught fish regularly during this period made the pattern obvious; had we only caught the occasional fish, the pattern might not have been evident.

My thoughts on all this are still evolving and I do not yet feel confident enough to make any dogmatic assertions, but I **am** confident enough to use what I have learned as a basis on which to formulate my baits.

In summer and autumn I use either particles, or home-made boilies made primarily from such ingredients as bird-foods, semolina, maize flour, soya flour and fish-meal. I would once have included meat and bone meal in that list, but since the BSE ("mad cow") scare am reluctant to even handle the stuff, let alone feed it to carp. Milk-products comprise no more than 30 per cent of the dry ingredients (by weight) of such mixes.

In late spring and early autumn, particularly if the weather is cool, I choose baits that contain 30 to 40 per cent milk products.

In winter proper and early spring, as well as in sudden cold snaps that occur any time after late October, I prefer to use baits with a 60 to 70 per cent milk-products content.

OTHER ADDITIVES

I keep changing my mind about oils. For a long while I used no extra oil in my bait (some ingredients, soya flour for example, contain quite a high oil or fat content) and caught plenty of carp on them. Then I wondered if my baits would be improved by the addition of sesame, olive, soya, sunflower or rapeseed oil—so I tried them, but cannot honestly say that such baits were either more or less effective. Currently I am in one of my ac d-oil phases, but not in the sort of quantities used in Premier-type fish-meal baits. That last comment is not to imply that I think there is anything wrong with high oil levels, because I do not know whether such is the case or not. I doubt it, unless oil-laden baits are used in such quantity that boilie-orientated carp in a hard-fished water develop almost total reliance on them.

I keep changing my mind about enhancers too. Actually the term "enhancers" is not as all-embracing as it seems. Some, particularly those used to enhance savoury flavours, are synthetic chemicals (eg monosodium glutamate); while sweet enhancers are often organically derived intense sweeteners (thaumatin being a good example). MSG has no inherent attraction, but intense sweeteners such as thaumatin appear to be attractive in their own right; so are they enhancers or attractors? Currently I add sweeteners to most of my mixes, so I also add sweet enhancers, usually a cocktail consisting of five drops of Cotswold's liquid Talin, five drops of their Liquid Milk Protein Sweet Enhancer (LMPSE) and five drops of their Reveal.

My favourite sweetener is Geoff Kemp's powder version, I usually add 2.5 ml to a pound (454 g) of dry mix. I may do this with what are regarded as savoury mixes too, those containing fish meal or liver powder for example.

Fish meal and liver powder are two of the taste-ingredients I commonly use to add to the bait's palatability and, hopefully, its acceptability. Others include molasses, honey, treacle, demerara cane sugar, dried yeast, mussel powder, squid powder, Robin Red and Colne Valley's Seafood Essence and Dutch Shrimp Additive. Sometimes these are used singly, but more commonly in combination; you will find details in the recipe section.

I have growing confidence in another of Colne Valley's products, Lactamino, which is a whey protein that has been pre-digested to an advanced degree and, according to the product-literature, contains approximately 25 per cent free-form amino acids that **may** provide a food signal. I am not **totally** convinced about the value of such products, but I err on the side of belief.

An additive in which I have decreasing confidence is vitamin-mineral supplement. I still tend to use it, but more as a legacy from my high-level milk-protein days than out of committed belief. Not only do I strongly suspect that vitamin-mineral supplements are unnecessary, but I worry about their palatability. I wonder too if sufficient vitamin content survives boiling to make their inclusion worthwhile anyway. I suspect that I may have bought my last tub of the stuff.

I realise that this chapter raises more questions than it answers, but as I said, my ideas are still evolving and it will not surprise me if they continue to do so for quite a long while to come.

Trouble is, the anomalies just won't go away. Neville Fickling summed it up rather nicely in an article in *Carpworld* (number eight) when he said, "In an ideal world, the theoretical understanding of carp nutrition should help us to formulate brilliant baits. Sadly, some of the best carp baits of all time are essentially rubbish if you care to analyse them!"

I am not sure to which baits Neville was referring; certainly few ready-mades qualify for that dismissive designation, as we have already seen. But the essence of what he said is true; our theoretical knowledge ought to enable us to produce superb baits, and should enable us to identify those that will be unsuccessful.

But it is not a perfect world; and carp frequently demonstrate preferences that appear to defy logic.

4 Boilie Making

Weighing out an ounce of this and half an ounce of that is a laborious chore, so I prepare bulk batches of dry-mix. I put the weighed-out ingredients into a plastic tub that is large enough to enable me to make five kilos of mix at a time. Having checked that the lid is secure I shake the tub vigorously until I am satisfied that the ingredients are thoroughly mixed. Some go further. Zen Bojko once told me that he and some friends hired a brand-new cement-mixer for the job; and this was in the days before he was a bait-tycoon!

The mixture is then bagged in strong poly-bags and labelled. Details of recipes, including any subtle variations from standard, are recorded in a notebook for future reference.

The appropriate number of eggs are cracked into a bowl and any liquid additives are whisked-in. Dry-mix is then trickled-in and stirred with a fork until the resulting dough becomes too stiff to stir further. Final kneading is done by hand. Sometimes I use a food-processor because it does the job brilliantly; but the extra washing-up is only justified if I am making a lot of bait.

Usually I use a bait-gun to extrude "sausages", but I find it advisable to make the dough a little softer than is ideal for rolling; otherwise the gun becomes very difficult to operate.

The slightly soft sausages are laid out on a large board and allowed to stand for a while, this causes them to firm-up somewhat as moisture within the dough is absorbed. When I judge the stiffness to be just right I put the sausages through a bait-roller. There are a number of rollers on the market but I get on best with the cheapest, which is Richard Gardner's version. I like the way his model has a built-in cutter and hand-grip.

Some mixes do not like rollers, and for those I use a bait-press. Despite their usefulness, they never became very popular and ceased production soon after their introduction. I would not be without mine, though.

Footnote: Recently I acquired a plastic roll-along-the-ground tub intended for mixing concrete; it has proved ideal for blending bulk dry-mixes. It cost about £24.

My bait-making kit: Gardner gun and rollers, measuring spoons and syringes. Presses, and mesh-bags for air-drying.

I like to have a selection of sizes in my freezer, but generally I use 18 mm boilies in summer, late spring and early autumn; and 14 mm or 16 mm baits in winter.

For close-range work I do not see the need for spherical boilies at all, so I often use boilie-cubes. These are gratifyingly simple to make and I can produce enormous quantities in a very short time. The dough should be a little stiffer than normal; and if it is folded and refolded it acquires a slightly open texture that results in slow-sinking, almost neutral-density baits. The stiff dough is rolled out into nice, firm rectangular slabs of the required thickness (usually about 10 mm). These are placed in the freezer for a quarter of an hour to harden, so they do not distort when cut into cubes. Like spherical boilies, they are placed in a bowl and rolled round in a small quantity of dry-mix to prevent them sticking together.

For boiling I use a chip-pan. It is three-quarters filled with water, brought to the boil and the baits are cooked in approximately five ounce (140 g) batches. It is important to be consistent in this respect or some will turn out softer than others. Boiling times depend on the mix and the bait-size. My cereal-based 18 mm baits are usually boiled for one

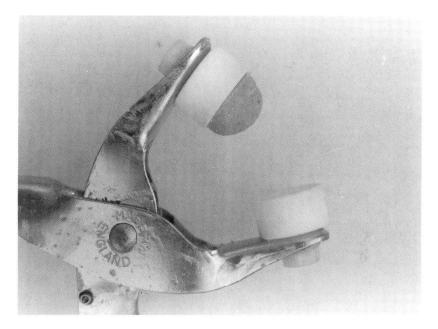

The bait-press never really caught on, but I like them. Here a boilie is moulded.

and a half minutes; smaller baits require correspondingly less time. Milk-proteins are boiled only until they pop to the surface, by which time they are skinned, but the inside remains largely uncooked. Excessive boiling will denature milk proteins which, I suspect, renders them less effective.

After boiling, baits are emptied out of the chip-pan cage into a colander to drain for a few minutes. They are then tipped onto a carp-sack in the garden and left to cool and dry. They may, at this point, be bagged up, labelled and put in the freezer. They may, on the other hand, be preserved by longer-term drying.

After drying for the appropriate length of time (two to four days, depending on the degree of dryness/hardness required), they are put in the freezer to prevent further dehydration, which would make them biscuity and brittle.

LONG-LIFE BOILIES

I first started thinking seriously about dried baits when I was told by a continental friend that he considered them superior to fresh ones. His enthusiasm for them was not influenced by their potential for longevity but, quite simply, because he considered them more effective. Obviously

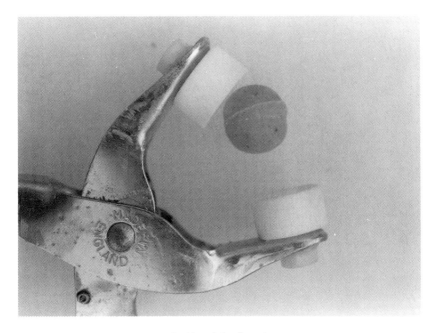

And here it is released.

I was interested in his reasoning but, to be honest, was not convinced that they could be superior. What very definitely **did** interest me, though, was the fact that dried baits would presumably stay "fresh" for long periods without there being any necessity to keep them chilled. For my normal day to day fishing the issue of bait freshness has never been a problem; but now and again I like to go for longer trips, maybe two days and nights at a stretch. And then there are the overseas trips. When I go to the continent for a solid week's fishing, there is no practical way of keeping baits fresh for the duration unless access to a freezer can be arranged. With this problem in mind my thoughts returned to my friend's dried baits. My lack of belief in their acceptability to carp was mitigated a little when I read Tony Davies-Patrick's comments about them—it seemed that he too rated them as not merely an alternative to fresh baits, but actually superior.

But try as I may, I had a mental-block about their use—it seemed illogical that dried baits could be as effective as fresh-thawed or freshly made baits. But what about "Munchies" and their ilk? They are dried "baits", and they work well enough. And I recalled Tim Paisley and, before him, Keith Sykes writing that HNV baits were at their most effective

Bird-food boilie-cubes. These are easy to make and I use them a lot.

for the first 24 hours from thawing (or less in very warm conditions), but then became effective after about 72 hours providing no mould had appeared. Tim and Keith were not talking about dried baits as such—but then three-day old baits are not exactly fresh either, are they?

So with a trip to France in the offing I decided to dry a kilo or so of fish-meal/bird-food/milk-protein baits that had been flavoured with bun-spice. The weather was hot and sunny at the time so I put the baits in a mesh bag and hung them on a tree in my garden. They stayed there for three days, baking in the full force of the sun. It went very much against the grain I can tell you—I had always taken great pains to keep my baits ultra-fresh, and here I was letting them broil in the midday sun! But I tried to rationalise what I was doing by telling myself that in many hot countries they preserve fish this way; and when I was in Africa I ate some biltong, I think it was called, which was dried antelope meat.

After their period of drying, the boilies were rock-hard. They smelled okay and looked okay—and when I dropped a few in water and left them for a few hours they reconstituted and struck me as being virtually identical to fresh-made baits.

I still was not convinced. Not until I caught a carp on them would

Bagging-up for freezing.

I be able to accept that they were a viable alternative to fresh baits. So I took them to France and fished them on one rod. On the other two rods I used boilies that had been made fresh on the bank. That night (it was a privately owned water and I had permission from the owner to night-fish) I caught five carp—three on the fresh-made boilies, two on the dried ones. "Mmmmm, interesting," I thought. I did not want to read too much into the distribution of captures, but it was fair to claim that the dried baits had at least held their own.

The next night I again used dried boilies on one rod and fresh-made baits on the other two. I had three carp that night—two of them fell to the dried baits.

"Mmmmm," I thought again, "**very** interesting!"

The first night could have been a fluke, but two nights on the trot ... things were looking decidedly promising. I had no further opportunity to try dried baits that trip for the simple reason that I had run out. But my confidence in their acceptability had moved a step or two in the right direction—but still there was a little "maggot" in my brain that gnawed away at wholehearted belief. My doubts went something like this, "Okay so they caught carp, they even held their own, more than held their own in fact, after all they were only used on one rod;

but these were easy, naive carp (and, as everyone knows **all** Continental carp are easy and naive!) ... perhaps they would not work with educated English fish."

The evidence that they worked on my home waters too came by accident. I made four kilos of bird-food/milk-protein baits flavoured with Geoff Kemp's Golden Syrup, as my back-up bait for a trip to Brittany; the first-line bait would be fresh-made each day. They were dried by being left for four days on newspaper on the floor of the spare bedroom (the weather was cool and damp at the time so I could not hang them out of doors). The trip fell through so there I was with a batch of bait that looked like it would sit unused in the bottom of my freezer. And so it remained until September, when number-two son was about to embark on a 24 hour session with his friend, Paul. I found Peter a batch of his favourite Scopex, and suggested he take a small bag of dried baits as spares.

I had given him plenty of Scopex baits, so he did not run short, but Paul did. "Try these," said Peter, handing his friend the dried ones.

Within 20 minutes or so of casting, Paul landed a 17 lb mirror!

Next trip Paul did not wait to run out of fresh baits, he used the dried ones at the outset and took another mirror of 19 lb 10 oz. Next time out he took a 14 lb common.

Not unnaturally that little episode reinforced my wavering confidence and helped persuade me that dried baits were worth a sustained trial. Subsequent experience has convinced me that they are a viable alternative to fresh baits, and will henceforth be my first choice for overseas trips; thus releasing me from the chore of bait-making whilst abroad and eliminating the need to try to arrange freezer-access.

While this was going on, I experimented with other methods of bait-preservation. I contacted several major food processing companies in the UK, and asked for advice about the use of chemical preservatives. I had several very interesting and helpful replies, and the general consensus seemed to be that potassium sorbate was the most likely candidate. The level recommended was 1/1000 (1 gm preservative to 1000 gm bait-mix).

I made up a milk-protein/bird-food mix containing the preservative in the recommended proportion, and first time out took a 25½ lb mirror on it. I subsequently learned that shop-bought shelf-like baits contain potassium sorbate, and at five or six times the level at which I used it; so obviously there can be no doubt about the palatability of baits incorporating it.

Which raises another point. Why bother to produce my own long-life baits for sessions and holiday trips? Why don't I do what most other anglers do and simply use shelf-life baits?

Footnote: Subsequent experience has reinforced my belief in the validity of dried baits; they are now my standard choice at home as well as abroad.

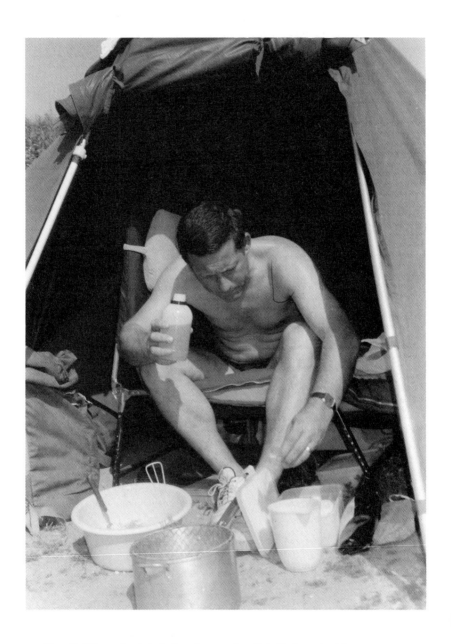

Geordie Mike makes bait during a long session. Dried baits make this unnecessary.

I have **always** made my own baits, I have confidence in them and, frankly, reckon them to be superior to any shop-bought alternatives. The fact that goodness-knows-how-many carp have fallen to shop-bought baits, does absolutely nothing to convince me that they are anything other than second best! Whether or not that is a correct assessment, or even a fair assessment, I honestly do not know—we are not talking logic and practicalities here, we are talking serious issues of confidence; or rather the lack of it!

I recently discussed this business of long-life baits with Rod Hutchinson, and for savoury baits he recommended using salt at the rate of 36 g per kilo of dry-mix. He said, "Don't worry that salt will put carp off, I think they like it."

Number-two son found a reference in his university library that seemed to endorse Rod's view, but Howard A. Loeb in his aforementioned experiments with food and flavours, found that salt evoked no reaction from carp at all; in fact there was no sign that they even detected it.

One of the problems of applying experimental evidence to bait formulation is that references are sometimes contradictory.

It might be worth mentioning that salt is sometimes used in commercially produced fish feeds to prolong freshness, as is propylene glycol. The reference came from *Nutrition and Feeding of Fish* by Tom Lovell (Van Nostrand Reinhold, New York) but I could find no details with regard to quantities required, so I do not know if our use of propylene glycol based flavours assists bait longevity.

POP-UPS

I am not a fan of those methods of making pop-ups that produce baits completely different in smell, taste and texture to those used as freebies. Mine are not, therefore, grilled, baked or micro-waved; instead they are made by the admittedly laborious procedure whereby mini poly-balls are incorporated inside each boilie. They are then boiled in the usual way. My pop-ups are therefore identical to my standard baits in every respect except buoyancy.

RECIPE SECTION

In the following recipes you will notice that I have not followed convention and given their protein percentage. This is because in isolation it is fairly meaningless, as it takes no account of the digestibility and quality of that protein. When you further consider that protein percentages **never** take account of the fact that egg solids (as distinct from total egg content)

Mini poly-balls; I prefer to incorporate these in my pop-ups, rather than use baked or micro-waved baits.

usually represent something like 15 per cent of a mix (by weight), and those solids have a protein content of about 50 per cent; it becomes obvious that the omission of such a significant protein source from the calculations makes a nonsense of the whole exercise. It is a valueless legacy from the days when we believed that high protein levels were inherently more attractive to carp, and would be recognised for their nutritional superiority.

They aren't, and they won't!

Now to specifics.

For most mixes I use fresh eggs, but occasionally I choose whole egg-powder instead. Both are equally effective as binders, but egg-powder produces baits that are slightly more dense; which may be an advantage in running water or for long-range freebie-baiting, but a disadvantage for fishing over silt.

If egg-powder is used I recommend that approximately one and a half ounces (42 g) be added to each 10 oz (280 g) dry-mix.

For mixes with a very high proportion of bird-food ingredients you will need about 115 ml liquid (inclusive of water, oils, flavours and liquid amino-additives etc) per 10 oz dry-mix.

Bait-making in the garden—here I can make a mess with impunity

Bird-food/milk-protein mixes require about 130 ml liquid per 10 oz; fish-meals will soak up a bit more, usually about 150 ml per 10 oz; and milk-protein mixes anything from 160 ml to 200 ml per 10 oz.

It is impossible to be precise because different ingredients absorb liquids at different rates; and anglers differ in how stiff they like their mixes to be. My guidelines should provide a useful starting point, though.

The amount of liquid in a fresh egg depends on the size; I always use size three eggs and they contain, on average, approximately 40 ml liquid. Rule-of-thumb guidelines for the number of fresh eggs per 10 oz mix therefore work out as follows:

bird-food mix: three eggs
bird-food/milk-protein mix: three to four eggs
fish-meal mix: four eggs
milk-protein mix: five eggs

First I shall give details of my milk-protein bulk-mix; this is the base I incorporate in most of my baits.

MILK-PROTEIN BULK BASE-MIX

1 kg 30 mesh Irish casein
1 kg 100 mesh acid casein
1 kg 90 mesh rennet casein
1 kg calcium caseinate or soluble milk-protein concentrate (Milk-Pro)
1 kg West German lactalbumin or soluble whey-protein concentrate (Whey-Pro)
1 kg egg albumen

Before giving individual recipes, and to avoid confusion, I should explain that when I use very small quantities of fine powders, I use volume measures (millilitres), because I find this easier and more accurate than trying to weigh them.

Larger quantities of powders are weighed in the normal way—and for conversion purposes remember that one ounce is 28 g.

MILK-PROTEIN HNV (winter, early spring, late autumn)

6 oz milk-protein base
2 oz soya flour (full-fat, heat-processed)
2 oz semolina
5 ml dried red blood cells and/or 5 ml dried yeast
10 ml Lactamino

5 ml olive oil

I have caught a lot of carp on this bait with no further additives. It also works well with low-level flavour, sweetener and my sweet enhancer cocktail.

Boil until baits rise to top of pan

For warmer weather I prefer the following recipes which have been very successful on a wide variety of waters both here and overseas.

BIRD-FOOD/MILK-PROTEIN (summer and autumn)

3 oz ground Nectarblend (or Red Factor Canary, or Sluis CLO etc)
2 oz milk-protein base mix
2 oz semolina
2 oz soya flour (full-fat, heat-processed)
1 oz Vitamealo
5 ml red blood cells and/or 5 ml dried yeast; or 1 oz Robin Red, or

1 oz white fish-meal
10 ml Lactamino
one heaped teaspoon demerara cane sugar

10 ml honey or molasses
10 ml olive oil

Boil for one and a quarter minutes to one and a half minutes.
10 ml Minamino plus enhancer cocktail and low-level flavour sprayed-on before freezing.

I adjust the mix according to time-of-year and water-temperature, by increasing the proportion of milk-protein in early spring and late autumn, and increasing the proportion of bird-food and cereal in high summer.

FISH-MEAL (summer and early autumn)

6 oz milk-protein base
3 oz mixed fish-meal (white, sardine, anchovy and capelin)
1 oz semolina
7 ml Dutch Shrimp Additive
10 ml Lactamino

15 ml sesame oil
10 ml Seafood essence

This bait is boiled for 45 seconds. It does not require heavy baiting as do some fish-meal mixes, in fact it caught well from its first introduction.

I realise that the proportion of milk-protein far exceeds my stated summer/autumn preference; but it works so well that I am disinclined to tamper with the recipe.

I was interested to read a couple of articles by Neville Fickling in which he said that in his opinion it was a waste of money using refined milk products like casein, and we would be better off using unrefined milk powder which was far cheaper. I bought some from the Moss/Fickling shop in Gainsborough and experimented with a few recipes. I found that milk powder could not be used as a direct substitute for casein etc, because it produced much softer baits; but I juggled with the recipes, and came up with a few mixes that produced good, firm baits and caught well.

BIRD-FOOD/MILK-PROTEIN (spring, summer and autumn)

3 oz Red Factor (or Sluis CLO, Nectarblend etc)
3 oz milk powder

1½ oz semolina
½ oz wheat gluten
1 oz egg albumen
1 oz Vitamealo
1 oz liver powder, plus 5 ml dried yeast; or 1 oz Robin Red
10 ml Lactamino
2.5 ml Kemp powder sweetener
1 ml Milk B enhancer (Cotswold)

10 ml sesame oil
    Boil for one and a quarter to one and half minutes.

10 ml Minamino, and low-level spray-on flavour before freezing

BIRD-FOOD/FISH-MEAL/MILK-PROTEIN (summer, early autumn)

2½ oz Sluis CLO
2½ oz milk powder
2 oz white fish-meal
2 oz semolina
1 oz wheat gluten
1 teaspoonful salt
5ml Dutch Shrimp Additive, plus 5 ml mussel extract, plus 5 ml dried
    yeast
10 ml Seafood Extract
5 ml rapeseed oil
10 ml Fish Feed Inducing Oil (Premier) or cod-liver oil

Boil for one and a quarter to one and a half minutes.

Earlier I mentioned a dried bait that I made for a French trip and which in limited use in the UK was encouragingly successful; here is the exact recipe:

DRIED SWEET-BIRDFOOD (spring, summer, autumn)

3 oz ground Nectarblend
3 oz milk-protein base
2 oz Vitamealo
1 oz semolina
½ oz wheat gluten
½ oz egg albumen

10 ml Lactamino
5 ml dried yeast
2.5 ml Kemp powder sweetener
1 ml Milk B (Cotswold)

10 ml liquid molasses
10 ml rapeseed oil
5 ml Golden Syrup flavour
   Boil for one and a half minutes. Dry for four days.

I could list dozens of other recipes, all of which have caught carp, but to be honest, I see little point—most are simply variations on a theme. If you like to experiment I suggest you obtain some bait-dealers' product catalogues; SBS, Premier, Nutrabaits and Cotswold all have detailed recipe sections. They contain a lot of ingredient information too, as does the excellent Colne Valley leaflet; and notwithstanding a certain amount of predictable product-hype, they are extremely informative publications.

An alternative to making your own mixes is, of course, to buy commercial ready-mixes. Some of these are very popular, proven mixes and have a lot of carp to their credit; but I am in no position to make recommendations because I have never used a pre-mix in my life.

A beautiful 19lb farm-reservoir common.

Mike and I fish a continental canal – and not another carp angler in sight.

This gorgeous 22 lb leather came from a big pit that links to the Seine.

My son reckons this picture "says it all". I agree with him.

Rick plays a French biggie. Michel casually looks on. The fish came off!

The water that produced Britain's record grass-carp, Ken Crow's Honeycroft Fishery.

This 27¾lb mirror failed to qualify as a winter fish by just one day!

5 Particles, Floaters and Others

If I gave a long list of particles it would be a deception because in truth I use a very small selection. I rate particles very highly, but only in summer and autumn. Yes, I know that some anglers have succeeded with them in winter, but not in very cold weather. One friend of mine who is something of a particle specialist, did very well on one big, deep water in the winter of 89/90; but the following winter he really struggled. You may recall that the winter of 89/90 was incredibly mild, down here in the south-east we only had one frost that I can recall; and overnight temperatures were often in or near low double-figures Centigrade. The winter of 90/91 was by no means a cold one, but we did have a week or two of snow cover, and quite a few nights when the temperature dipped below zero. It came closer to being a normal winter, and that, in my opinion, is why my particle-fishing friend had such a lean time.

NUTS

The most effective particles are arguably nuts; they are unusual in that they seem to retain their appeal, even after a lot of fish have been caught on them. Unfortunately there is a downside to all this, and nuts have been blamed for carp losing condition and, in some cases, dying. Used correctly and sparingly nuts are **not** harmful, but undeniably there has been abuse and misuse, and in some waters carp have unquestionably suffered as a consequence. Problems occur on two levels: too many anglers using too many nuts leads to a level of preoccupation which, evidence suggests, results in serious vitamin deficiency; and the use of uncooked nuts has undoubtedly been responsible for carp deaths due to ingested baits swelling in the carp's gut and becoming jammed solid.

The most effective are probably peanuts, especially the large jumbo variety. They can be obtained from pet shops or bird-food suppliers. Take care only to buy food-quality nuts that are guaranteed free of toxic

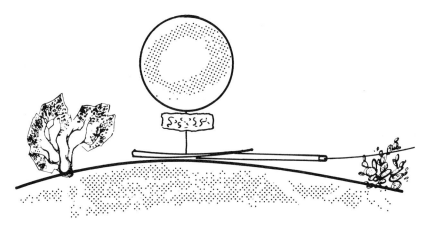

Fig. 18. Pop-up hazel nut.

fungi, because there is a question mark over the safety of some allegedly condemned nuts that may find their way onto the market.

Next, and many believe as good as peanuts, are tiger nuts. Supplies of these have been erratic for the last year or two, but when obtainable you can get them from health food shops and from some tackle shops.

Few other nuts are used to any significant extent, certainly not by me, although carp have been caught on hazel nuts, almonds and brazils. They can all be bought from supermarkets, but are rather expensive— which has the hidden advantage that it prevents over-use. They tend to be used mainly to overcome peanut and tiger nut bans; although increasingly these days we are encountering blanket-bans on all nuts.

Hazel nuts and brazils are almost neutral density so are useful for fishing on silty or weedy bottoms; in fact a proportion of hazels are floaters, so with the addition of a small piece of rig-foam can be used pop-up style (Fig 18).

Brazils can be used whole, but I understand they also work well when each nut is cut into two or three smaller pieces.

Almonds are taken enthusiastically, I am told, but their shape makes it impossible to catapult them any great distance; so they are only really suitable for the margins and just beyond. They obviously work, though. There is a small water near my home that is occupied throughout the school summer holidays by a small group of pre-pubescent, bivvy-bound youngsters; all of whom seem to have the pond's resident thirty-pounder to their credit, which invariably falls to almonds.

Some anglers believe that carp have to be weaned onto nuts by pre-baiting; this is not so, they will be taken from the outset. A pound or so (450 gm) of cooked nuts is sufficient for a day or night's fishing, even when the carp are well on feed. There is absolutely no need to use nuts by the bucketful. Two or three pouches catapulted round each hookbait at the commencement of a session is sufficient, while a further couple of pouches may be put out after a run.

In this context I would like to mention that when I fished the West Warwick Reservoir at Walthamstow, the most successful anglers by far were a pair from, I think, Brentwood. We never actually spoke beyond a mutual nodded "Good morning," so I know very little about them other than the fact that they were superb particle anglers. They carried the minimum of gear, and spent a lot of time wandering the banks of the reservoir searching for carp. When they saw signs, or came to a spot that by virtue of their knowledge of the water they knew was worth a try, they would very quietly set up and, in contrast to those who think the only way to fish nuts is to fill-in with them, would just put two or three pouches round each bait.

Due to their mobility, their ability to set up quietly and their careful use of feed, no one came near them in terms of number of carp caught. They were pretty to watch.

I subsequently learned that they had obtained season tickets for Savay, and I said to Rick that I thought they would do very well there. But whether they were intimidated by Savay's reputation and adopted the approach used by everyone else, or had their mobility restricted by too many pitches having anglers in them, I do not know. But they evidently substituted banging-out-the-boilies for the approach that they had developed to something approaching an art-form. Predictably they did not catch much; which is a shame because if they had "done it their way", as the song goes, I am convinced they would have been very successful.

Preparation

All nuts should be soaked for at least 24 hours, then brought to the boil and simmered for 30 minutes for tigers, 20 minutes for the others. There is no need to use a pressure-cooker, an ordinary saucepan is perfectly suitable. Do not, incidentally, expect tiger nuts to go soft; they remain hard no matter how long they are cooked.

Some anglers add a few drops of concentrated boilie sweetener to the water in which nuts are soaked; carp undoubtedly have a "sweet tooth" and seem to appreciate the taste, but that said, they like unsweetened, unflavoured nuts too.

Black-eyed beans.

BLACK-EYE BEANS

Rod Hutchinson introduced me to these in the very early days of particles, before they had received widespread publicity. They were an excellent bait, and still are. They are accepted instantly and carp obviously like them. Given the opportunity carp will eat quite large quantities of black-eyes, in fact it sometimes seems that a fair bed of them is needed in a pitch before carp will display interest. Two to four ounces (56 g to 112 g) round each hook-bait is a sensible and effective level at which to use them; although in heavily stocked waters much larger quantities can be used and carp will clear them readily.

You can buy black-eyes from most supermarkets, or failing that try shops that specialise in Indian food.

Preparation

Black-eyes are best prepared as per Rod's original recommendation, which is by soaking for 12 hours in double-strength tomato soup (made by mixing two packets of tomato soup powder with the amount of water

Chick-peas.

recommended for one packet); then bringing to the boil and simmering gently for about 20 minutes.

CHICK PEAS

These are among the heaviest and most aerodynamic of the particles, so can be catapulted further than can most other mass baits. They are obviously highly palatable and carp will eat them in quantity. I recommend they be used in similar quantity to that recommended for black-eyes.

They are not suitable for fishing over foul-smelling silt because they take up external flavours so readily, and after sitting on silt for a relatively short time will lose their natural smell and acquire a distinctive, and unappetising silt smell. I have never caught a carp on baits contaminated in this way.

Preparation

Their inclination to take on external smells and flavours can be used to good effect in that chick peas can readily be sweetened and flavoured.

As a general guide, I recommend that 5 ml of solvent-based boilie flavour and 2.5 ml liquid sweetener be added to the water in which a kilo of baits is soaked for 24 hours. They should then be brought to the boil and simmered for 20 minutes. This method will produce beautifully flavoured baits. But, as with nuts, they do not need this treatment to be rendered acceptable, because carp obviously like them plain.

MAPLE-PEAS

Unlike black-eyes and chick-peas, maples are very resistant to contamination, which means that they are difficult, if not impossible, to flavour or sweeten. It also means that they are excellent for fishing over foul-smelling silt, because they will retain their natural taste.

They work well in small to medium quantities, two ounces (56 g) round each hookbait is about right. In heavily stocked waters this quantity can obviously be increased considerably, and when a large group of carp really get their heads down on maples it can be almost impossible to overbait; but generally I recommend erring on the side of caution and baiting fairly lightly.

Preparation

Some anglers favour fermented maples, and after cooking leave them standing in the cooking water for several days until it goes milky. I have never used them prepared this way, so cannot vouch for their effectiveness. I prefer to give them a 12 hour soak, bring them to the boil and simmer for 20 minutes.

TARES

I rarely use these as hookbait, but often use them as feed in conjunction with other particles, especially hempseed. They are relatively resistant to taking on flavours so are generally cooked in plain water, although I think it is worth adding a few millilitres of liquid sweetener. They require a 12 hour soak, after which they are brought to the boil and simmered for 20 minutes.

HEMPSEED

Possibly **the** particle for holding fish in a pitch, and encouraging them to re-visit a pitch after they have moved off. Carp do not just pick at hempseed the way they sometimes do with other particles; they really work the bottom with enthusiasm, and will turn over stones and suck at crevices to get at the last remaining seeds. Ken Townley gave an enlightening and fascinating account of this behaviour in a marvellous article, "Looking In On Carp", which appeared in *Coarse Angler* in October 1989.

Enthusiastic feeding on hempseed can be a disadvantage, because carp sometimes get so preoccupied that they will ignore boilies or other baits in the same pitch. Although hempseed **can** be used as hookbait, it is not something I have ever managed to do successfully. It is better, I think, to use tares as hookbait under these circumstances.

Preparation

Hemp should be soaked for 12 hours, then brought to the boil and simmered very gently for 35 to 40 minutes. You can tell when it is cooked because a white shoot appears.

My Belgian friends, who have a long pedigree when it comes to using hempseed, in fact it was the Belgians who introduced the bait to the UK in the first place, tell me that it should be germinated before being cooked. Germination is evidently achieved by keeping the seeds damp, and waiting until the white shoot appears—this takes a few days in warm weather. Only then, they tell me, should it be cooked. I explained that we in UK would not be able to prepare it this way, because our hempseed is treated (I presume it to be by irradiation), to prevent it germinating. This, I learned from some long-forgotten source, is to prevent marijuana plants taking over from tomatoes as the UK's favourite garden crop! That may be so. But last summer I inadvertently spilled some presoaked hempseed on my lawn whilst tipping it into a saucepan for boiling and, treated or not, some decidedly strange-looking plants pushed their way up through the grass. The Flymo intervened and prevented a swoop by the drugs squad!

So presumably, not all our hemp is treated to make it sterile, and we can use the Belgian method of preparation if we so wish.

MAIZE

Not very highly rated by most UK anglers, yet very popular on the continent. My trials suggest that although carp take it, its continental popularity probably has more to do with availability and cheapness than with a particularly high level of attractiveness. It is a hard bait but, despite that, is more readily taken by bream than you would expect.

The maize generally available in UK and on the continent is the hard, yellow sort; but far better is the white, sweet African variety. This is not readily available in UK, but is sometimes obtainable from shops in areas that are tenanted by large numbers of West Indians. It is much softer than yellow maize, and carp obviously like it. Trouble is, bream and tench like it even more. Not just sizeable bream either, even small ones will peck away at it until they have left an empty husk.

I was discussing the attractiveness of white maize with a bait-buff friend of mine, and he said, "That's because it has a high lysine content."

To quote Mandy Rice-Davies's immortal words, "He would say that, wouldn't he?"

I suggested to my friend that its appeal might simply be due to the fact that carp like the taste.

He was dismissive of such a naive suggestion; as indeed I expected him to be.

Bait-buffs are like that!

Whatever the reason for its appeal, carp take it first time of seeing it. In fact it is at its best during initial sessions, before bream and tench get a taste for it.

OTHERS

Groats have become popular in recent seasons, particularly in the north-west of the country; but I have never used them, and to be honest do not even know what a groat looks like. I recall reading an article by Paul Selman in which he said that groats are the one particle that should not be cooked, they merely have to be soaked, and will evidently absorb flavours readily.

It is a strange name though ... "Groat" ... sounds more like a skin disfigurement than a bait!

The success of sweetcorn has been well documented over the years, and although neglected nowadays, will undoubtedly catch carp in the right circumstances. Number-two son's friend, Paul, had a twenty-plus mirror last summer on margin sweetcorn; and that from a water that was flogged to death with corn during the era when the world and his wife, son, dog, cat and budgie used the stuff. Just goes to show. I always carry a tin or two in the boot of my car, but have not actually used it as hookbait for at least two years.

In *Big Water Carp* I mentioned that soya beans were not a particularly successful particle bait, and I had serious doubts about their palatability. After reading that comment, Colin Booker, of Colne Valley Baits, con-tacted me to tell me that on a couple of waters fished by him and his brother Tony, soya beans had been the most successful particle bait of them all! There are, it appears, exceptions to every "rule"!

I wonder though, if my experience with soya beans was with them in their natural state; and Colin and Tony's was with heat-treated beans? The reason I ask is because I recently read in Tom Lovell's *Nutrition and Feeding of Fish*, that roasted soya beans are more palatable, and therefore more readily taken by fish, than they are in their unroasted form. This is when they are used as commercial feed, but surely it would apply to angling as well?

The only other particles I shall mention are maggots and casters. Both are highly rated by carp, and in waters where heavy weed does not hamper effective presentation, and unwanted species do not render their use untenable, they can be very effective. I know a lot of Redmire fish fell to maggots and casters way back in the 60's, and the approach has been used there with success by my friend, Steve Edwards, very recently.

It is also worth bearing in mind that in pre-pole days (what God-awful, unwieldy monstrosities they are—talk about taking a sledge-hammer to crack a nut!), when a lot of matchmen used hemp and casters in combination, carp were frequently hooked, and occasionally landed, in rivers that held them. On Layer too, slow-sinking maggots on a long tail produced some terrific bags of carp. Not baby carp either, such as are caught in those over-stocked Mickey Mouse waters that are full of dear little hand-sized mirrors, but fish to double-figures. Mind you, on being caught they were crammed into keepnets. I got criticised in the Press for writing in my book *Tench* (Beekay) that the banning of keepnets would be a major conservation measure. So I will say it again. **No** fish, of any size or species, should be put in a keepnet. There is no such thing as a safe keepnet, especially when relatively large catches are retained. As for catches of Layer-size carp being kept in them—only someone with a brain the size of a lentil would even consider anything so stupid and irresponsible.

Offended parties can now have another "go"!

FLOATERS

On thinking about this section, before sitting down to write it, it occurred to me that I do far less floater fishing than I used to, and I wondered why. Then I remembered—birds! Most of my fishing these days is done in big waters, and on those waters birds are an absolute pain. Don't get me wrong, I like to watch the antics of water-birds as much as does the next man (liar!), but they **are** a nuisance. No sooner do I put out a piece of anchored floater, than the surface is furrowed by birds surging towards it, and the sky is full of wheeling, squealing gulls. "Why not pull the floater just below the surface?" you might wonder.

Ha ha!

Birds that can find a solitary 14 mm boilie at the bottom of 30-plus feet of water in the vastness of a squillion acre pit, have **no** trouble finding a piece of floater pulled a few inches below the surface!

Floater fishing is viable in smaller waters though, because most water birds have a sort of minimum distance they are prepared to approach a visible angler. If you fish within that distance, the bird-problem can be minimised quite considerably. Incidentally, did you know that hanging a carp-sack in a tree adjacent to your pitch will, on a windy day when the sack blows and flaps, ensure that water birds do not come within 50 yards or so of you? That can help matters whether you are fishing bottom or surface baits.

If water birds and gulls allow you to fish floating baits, you can use either dried dog-food like Chum Mixer, or floater-cake made to the following recipe:

7 oz milk-protein base
1 oz gluten
1 oz soya-flour
1 oz semolina
2 teaspoons baking powder
2.5 ml Kemp powder sweetener
pinch yellow powder food-dye

25 ml Kemp Mellow Brandy

Add the above mixture to 12 size three eggs, and pour into a pre-greased non-stick baking-tin.

Place on the middle shelf of a pre-heated oven at gas Mk 2 (electric 300) and cook for one and a quarter hours.

Do not worry about the seemingly high flavour level; most of it evaporates off during cooking, and the high initial level is to compensate for that fact.

Floater-cake freezes well, so I make several "loaves" before the season starts, cut them into manageable slices, then bag and freeze them. And they are usually still there at the end of the season because, as stated earlier, I do hardly any floater fishing these days!

OTHERS

A lot of other baits will catch carp, for example: worms, luncheon-meat, trout pellets, salmon pellets, pet-food paste, sausage-meat paste, bread.

Bread!

Not one of my favourites I admit; but having watched Brian Mills creeping and crawling round weedy corners and bays, and winkling out carp on float-fished bread on days when no one else managed a take, I am tempted to revise my opinion. I do not think I will throw my boilies in the bin though, because in the case of anglers like Brian, their success is due (if I may borrow an old movie title) to the singer, not the song.

6 Groundbaiting and Prebaiting

There is a lot of anecdotal evidence relating to the value of groundbaiting, and the quantities we should use.

And most of it is contradictory!

Some successful anglers recommend very large amounts; Martin Locke, in his seed-mix adverts, has said that anglers are currently using up to two dozen eggs worth every 24 hours. How many actual boilies that represents depends on the type of mix used and the size of the baits, but for 18 mm bird food boilies, I reckon it is upwards of 1000. Martin went on to say that when he caught Savay's Sally, it was over a bed of 3000 one inch (about 25 mm) baits.

Others subscribe to the opposite view and use comparatively little, sometimes none at all; particularly in waters where a lot of bait is put in by other anglers. Kevin Maddocks has documented several instances of success with very light or non-baiting under such circumstances.

I suppose I lean towards the use-it-sparingly school, but accept the fact that there are undoubtedly times when a large bed of baits works best. The simple truth is that there is doubtless a case for heavy baiting on occasions, and an equally good case for very light baiting at other times. In other words, there is no universal best approach.

To some extent it must depend on the sort of fishing we do. I am not a session-man; and that has probably influenced my perceptions as regards the amount of bait that should be used. Were I the sort who bivvied-up for several days at a stretch, maybe I would see large quantities of bait in a more favourable light. Until two seasons ago I was a committed high-level milk-protein user, and I think that is an important factor too — but I will enlarge on the possible significance of that presently.

Time of year is important; few of those who recommend heavy baiting continue to do so in winter. I am talking here of ordinary, unwarmed stillwaters; certainly some successful Trent carp anglers continue to feed heavily in winter, as do those who fish artificially warmed stretches of canal and river, both here and on the continent.

Whether it is possible to see groundbaiting and prebaiting as separate entities, or if they are inseparably part of the same equation, I am not sure. I am tempted to think that they can work both independently and as complementary components of a whole.

A bed of attractive, palatable baits might indeed encourage browsing carp to seek them out and feed with greater enthusiasm than they otherwise might have done. And once a few carp start feeding, there is a lot of evidence to suggest that this can encourage others to do likewise. We **may**, therefore, transform what would have been a modest feeding spell into a very active one. The difference, perhaps, between a fish or two, and a multiple catch?

On the other hand, if one or two carp are in a "picking" mood, and they move into a heavily baited pitch, they might only pick up the odd bait, and the chances of the hookbaits being among them are statistically slim. Too many freebies, in this instance, making the difference between one or two fish, and a blank, maybe?

On yet other occasions carp will move into an area and, whilst not actively seeking food, can be stimulated into feeding by the presence of a fairly large quantity of it. I remember Rod Hutchinson describing how a couple of quite large fish moved over a bed of black eyes he had put down in a margin swim in Johnson's Railway Lake. When they came upon the bait, they tipped up and started feeding, but only until they had thinned out the beans a bit; then they moved off.

More beans in the pitch stimulated renewed interest and feeding; but again, only until they had been thinned once more. This frustrated Rod, because the fish never cleared enough beans to make it likely that the hook-bait would be found.

Can we predict what will happen, and feed accordingly? To a degree, I think we can. If conditions look good, a big, mellow south-westerly for example, I think we can be reasonably optimistic that carp might feed with enthusiasm. A case for a big bed of bait, perhaps? But if conditions look less promising, and are unlikely to result in a lot of active carp in the area, it surely makes sense to feed sparingly.

In betwixt-and-between conditions, neither particularly good nor particularly poor, I would err on the side of caution, and not feed heavily; but I would want enough bait to hopefully stimulate interest, and maybe encourage wandering carp to make return visits.

Timing is important too. If carp are already in the swim, and evidence of this might be provided by leaping and rolling, I think it is foolish to bombard the area with baits. But if we arrive early morning, and the forecast is for a big wind springing up after an hour or two, we might profitably put out a fair bed of bait, so it is there in readiness for the anticipated arrival of the carp.

Although I said that we should not bait on top of fish, I can recall occasions when they were feeding so enthusiastically that it made no difference at all. I remember a 22 lb leather that plucked my indicator from my fingers as I was attaching it to the line, having just recast after landing a 19 pounder!

I remember too Rick telling me about a day when he caught 20-odd carp from Layer on particles; he waded out on a shallow spit to bait-up heavily, and several times had a run as he paddled back to his rods! He reckoned he might have caught more fish, but he only had a bucketful of baits with him and ran out!

But instances such as those are exceptions, and should not be seen as ideal models for groundbaiting technique.

I have often said that I do not think groundbait will attract carp to an area in which they would otherwise not have gone. I do, however, think it can persuade them to return to an area that they have vacated. I have watched this happen in the close-season, and seen how carp will feed for a while, perhaps clearing up all the baits, perhaps not, then leave the area and return a short time later, looking for more. Sometimes, interestingly, they have one or two extra carp for company when they return. I do not know for sure that this sort of thing happens in non-observable situations; but then again I have no reason to think that it does not.

Semi-connected with the subject of groundbaiting is that of stringers. I nearly always incorporate a two or three bait stringer (Fig 19), only dispensing with it if I want to achieve maximum casting range. I like to use a stringer because, to repeat something I wrote in *Big Water Carp*, I think it amplifies the nutritional signal. That signal might be visual, it might be smell and taste, it might be touch; but more likely will be a combination of those. Put simply, I believe it increases the chance of the bait being found.

Stringers have an incidental, but nonetheless worthwhile advantage, in that they reduce the risk of tangles. In practice, it means that a good rig becomes, with the addition of a stringer, virtually 100 per cent snarl-proof. I find that fact comforting, and it enables me to fish with greater confidence.

The practice of fishing boilies over particles became a very in-vogue thing to do when milk-protein baits were more popular than they are today. I am becoming increasingly convinced that the main advantage of this approach was that carp fed far more enthusiastically on the particles than they would have on a big bed of milk-protein baits.

Number two son had an experience that lends weight to that view. He told me that last summer, when he lightly baited a margin-pitch with side-by-side patches of maple peas and mid-level milk-proteins, he watched carp clear-up the maples, and then swim off without so much

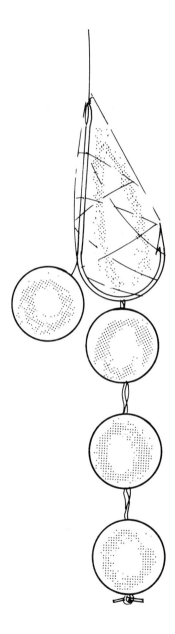

Fig. 19. Three bait stringer. I like to sheathe the hook in PVA tape to reduce yet further the risk of tangles, and to ensure that the hook does not hang-up on weed.

Number-two son fishes a big gravel-pit.

as a glance at the boilies! This evidently happened on a number of occasions.

The boilies over particles technique became less popular with the increased use of fish-meal and bird-food based boilies, due in part, no doubt, because they were cheaper than milk-proteins, but also because anglers found that carp fed far more enthusiastically over them than they ever did over milk-protein baits.

As already mentioned, so called "crap baits" contain ideal levels of protein and energy ingredients for optimum growth. They are also highly palatable, and very digestible. So not surprisingly, carp respond well to such baits when they are used for long-term prebaiting.

Some anglers argue that anything introduced in quantity will, if it is palatable and edible, be taken enthusiastically. Not true. Try it with potatoes or water-bound boiled dough-balls. Runs will occur in inverse proportion to the amount put in. Carp "like" potatoes and dough-balls in that they take them readily first time of encountering them; but prebaiting with them kills their effectiveness stone dead. I am tempted to conclude that this is because prebaiting enables carp to recognise that, nutritionally, such baits are poor. But that argument does not withstand scrutiny when

one considers how well nuts work; so it is one of those things that just
has to be accepted at face value—even though the reason is not understood.

It is also tempting to conclude that the reason soya/semolina/bird-
food/fish-meal (in whatever combination) baits work so well, is that they
are nutritious, digestible and taste good. Which may indeed be true, but
does not explain why milk-proteins are much less effective when baited
heavily.

Martin Locke has described how he and other successful anglers
concluded that the reduced success with milk-proteins they were exper-
iencing, was due to carp associating such ingredients with danger. This
is an improbable explanation, because individual fish are caught far more
often nowadays on fish-meal and bird-food baits, than they ever were
on milk-proteins. More likely the reduced effectiveness of milk-proteins
was due simply to the fact that as they became more popular, more went
in; and they just do not withstand volume baiting.

Some, wanting to be "scientific" to the last, have concluded that
protein-satiation occurs when milk-protein HNV's are baited in quantity.
I have even read a reference to "protein-overload", whatever that may
be.

I have refrained from suggesting actual quantities, because what is
right for one situation, will be completely wrong for another. It depends,
as already mentioned, on weather conditions, time of year, length of stay
and, quite obviously, the number and size of carp in the water. We might
have to consider nuisance fish too. So I will end this discussion on groundbaiting by quoting something I have said many times before: if you are
in the wrong spot, no amount of groundbait will help you; if you are
in the right spot, you will catch with very little. That is not to say that
groundbaiting will not make a good swim better; but equally it might
make a mediocre swim worse. Getting it right requires judgement, luck
and 20/20 foresight!

Now, what about prebaiting? Is it worthwhile?

I have to say that I have undertaken quite a few pre-baiting campaigns
with milk-protein baits, and whilst I have often caught carp after doing
so, I have **never** felt that my results have been commensurate with the
amount of time, effort and expense involved. Indeed, I have been as successful with milk-protein baits on using them completely new to a water,
as I have after prebaiting. Probably more so, in fact.

By contrast, a number of years ago Len Burgess and I had a dramatic
run of success on three different pits, after pre-baiting with a fish-pellet
based bait. That bait too was successful when used without prebaiting;
but there is little doubt in either Len's mind or mine that our baiting
programmes resulted in us catching far more fish than we otherwise would
have done.

After initial introductions in identified key feeding areas, we each put out about two pounds of golf-ball size boilies, 24 hours before each night trip.

We were fishing different waters at the time, and after these one-nighters, would ring each other to ask not, "Did you catch?" but "How big, and how many?"

My subsequent conversion to milk-protein baits was, predictably, accompanied by the adoption of the same baiting policy. But as already stated, try as I may, I cannot recall a single instance of a baiting campaign with milk-protein baits proving really effective.

Whilst there are doubtless a number of readers thinking that I am mistaken; I bet there are far more who are nodding in agreement.

Objective comparison is impossible, because I cannot be certain that when I did well on fish-pellet baits, I would not have done equally well, or even better, on milk-proteins. Similarly, when milk-based baits were disappointing, I have no way of knowing that fish-pellet would have been any better. But I am nonetheless left with the overriding impression that prebaiting with milk-proteins is at best a waste of time, and may actually be counter-productive.

My future policy, in both UK and on the continent, will be to prebait and groundbait with baits consisting primarily of cereal products like bird-food, soya flour and semolina. Milk products will be included in relatively small quantities, (as discussed in the recipe section), and I am inclined to Neville Fickling's view that this may as well take the form of ordinary milk-powder.

The extent to which I think long-term pre-baiting is useful depends on what we are trying to achieve. Whilst I do not think it is necessary to pre-bait with a new bait to get it established, because good baits are taken instantly, I am convinced that long-term baiting can only make a good bait better.

Only on very lightly fished waters would I consider baiting-up specific swims; for I see little point investing money, time and effort in a baiting programme, if early success leads to my finding someone's bivvie stuck there ever after! If the water is a quiet one I might consider swim-baiting, but only if I am convinced that those swims are in carp-favoured areas. I do not believe we can persuade carp to feed in swims that they otherwise would not have chosen; but regular baiting of areas that they favour anyway, might heighten their expectations of finding our bait there, and may encourage more frequent visits than might otherwise be the case.

In this context it is interesting how anglers who have visited some of the more popular continental waters like Cassein, Salagou and the River Lot, have reported how fishing was initially slow, but improved after three or four days when a swim was kept constantly and heavily baited. I would, however, caution against placing too much reliance on baiting, because even on well stocked waters like Salagou, it is not enough to simply fill-in and wait; as innumerable anglers who have blanked by so doing will testify. You have to find an area that carp visit on a regular basis, preferably one in which they feed by choice, regardless of whether or not there is any bait there. Bait alone, will not do the job for you.

A strange situation sometimes occurs on heavily stocked continental waters, where the carp are not yet particularly bait-orientated. Heavy baiting can be followed by large numbers of carp rolling in the pitch; but no takes. The rolling might continue on and off for several days, which not surprisingly encourages anglers to sit tight and wait for the carp to start "having it". But the runs do not happen.

Very frustrating. Baffling too. I wonder what makes carp behave this way?

The bait-buffs, of course, have the answer—attractor overload.

That's a belter, isn't it?

I wish I'd thought of it!

An alternative to swim-baiting is to bait-up on a general scatter principle over the whole water. This is practical on small waters, but obviously cannot be done on big pits and lakes unless several anglers share the cost and effort. Even then, there comes a point when it is just not a practical proposition. It can, however, happen unintentionally when a certain sort of bait becomes popular on a water. Take Premier-type fish-meals, for example. Word gets around that these are producing well, so everyone chucks in loads of them. Although individual anglers are only baiting their own swims, taken together it amounts to volume-baiting of the whole lake. Perhaps because the baits are highly palatable and, due to their similarity to commercial fish-feeds, presumably very digestible and nutritious, carp become enthusiastic about them. Where massive quantities are used, I think it likely that a proportion of carp in the water may even become partially dependent on them.

The same thing happens with ready-mades such as Richworth's Tutti Fruttis or Tropicanos; perhaps for the same reasons.

With the right bait it should be possible for a small group of anglers to achieve the same effect for themselves. Actually, I **know** it is. But that is someone else's story, and not for me to tell.

I realise that my constant references to digestibility and nutritional quality do not stand up against the indisputable success of nuts. I am not going to dismiss that as a mere aberration, and forget it. There **is** a reason for the effectiveness of nuts, but it seems most improbable that it has anything to do with nutritional worth or digestibility. Until we find out why they work so well, if indeed we ever do, we will just have to accept their undoubted appeal as a fact, and not run round in circles trying to manipulate our neat theories so the anomalies can be accommodated.

Cobra sticks, Cobra Groundbaiter, Boilie Caddy, Gardner Bait-Rocket, Black Widow 'pult and pouch 'pult.

GETTING IT THERE

I have, in the past, said some pretty unkind things about throwing-sticks.

I take it all back!

I have since acquired a couple of Cobras, and can get baits **at least** as far as I can with a wrist-rocket type catapult. They have a distinct advantage when fishing against a facing wind, because with practice I find that baits can be sort of thrown "under the wind" in a very flat trajectory that out-performs any catapult. I particularly like the King Cobra, and find the extra length seems to suit my technique.

A throwing-stick can, with practice, also be used to put out a group of boilies; but I do not find it as accurate in this respect as is a pouch catapult.

Nine Sansome, the lady who designed the Cobra throwing-sticks, recently sent me her Boilie-Caddy to try. It is a sort of ever-open "bum-bag" for holding boilies while groundbaiting. It is a useful item for any baiting situation, but a real boon when wading out to do it. Certainly it permits slicker and faster baiting than is possible with boilies stuffed in pockets.

Mike whacks 'em out.

Not that its usefulness is confined to boilies; it facilitates particle-baiting too.

For mass-baiting with either boilies or particles, at distances of up to 30 or 40 yards (depending on bait-size), Cobra's Groundbaiter is excellent. It is superb for groundbait balls too; which brings me to the next technique I want to mention.

When I have fished in France, I have been struck by a groundbaiting technique that my French friends use a lot. They pack balls of clay with as many particles and chopped boilies as possible, then catapult them out to the fishing area. I have not tried it with clay, but have used layers' mash; and in conjunction with a Groundbaiter, found it a very efficient way of getting particles out up to 50 or 60 yards.

An alternative is a bait-dropper. Just as I was impressed with my French friends' clay-balling technique, they were impressed with the efficiency of a bait-dropper. Which, in case Bob Morris is wondering, is why I buy so many of them. I have to replace those I leave with continental friends! Talking of Bob Morris reminds me that recently, on buying yet another bait-dropper, a Gardner Bait-Rocket actually, Bob asked, 'Do you use it as it is, or do you pull a condom over it?'

Alain prepares clay-balls.

"Why would I want to do that?" I asked.
"It's called safe-spodding," said Bob!
I walked right into that one, didn't I?

Gardner's Bait-Rocket is far superior to the home-made ones that I used to make from Fairy Liquid containers. This was shortly after I was introduced to them by Mark Vogelsang. I cannot recall if Mark actually invented "spods", but his was certainly the first I ever saw.

A couple of anglers, who I only knew as "The Twins", were very successful on one of my local pits, due to their having developed "spodding" to a high level of expertise. They were, by reputation, capable of putting out particles near the 100 yard mark. I cannot vouch for that fact, because when I watched them in action they were achieving a range of between 70 and 80 yards; which is still one hell of a long way to bait with particles! They used beachcasters and big, sea-size fixed-spool reels, in conjunction with relatively fine line and heavy shock-leaders, to hurl out their spods. It must have been hard work though. I have never "spodded" at the sort of range achieved by The Twins, but building up a bed of particles at even medium range is an exhausting business;

Mike baiting-up with chicks for Alain!

I am going to eat, even if the carp show little inclination to do so!

not to mention the numb-with-pain forefinger due to frequent and excessive line pressure across it.

It can, however, be worth the discomfort. Although Geordie Mike might question that fact. I recall with amusement the time he spent upwards of an hour spodding with chick-peas on a big French pit, only to have Alain, in the next pitch along, stack up carp like the proverbial breeze-blocks—every one of which spewed up masses of Mike's chick-peas!

Next evening, Alain asked Mike if he was going to bait-up for him again . . .

I don't know what Mike replied because it was in Geordie. It definitely sounded rude though!

7 Margins, Snags and Surface

To an ever-increasing number of anglers, as I have already intimated, carp fishing means bivvying-up for several days at a stretch, having first piled in the bait.

So deeply is session-fishing ingrained in modern carp fishing culture, that many are reluctant to fish in any other manner. Indeed, waters that have a night-fishing ban are usually much less hard-fished than those where it is allowed.

The emphasis on session-fishing has led to a gradual change in the strategy and approach used by most anglers. It has also led to a massive support industry in the provision of superb comfort-accessories, culminating in "man at Kevin Nash", as Paul Selman wittily put it. But these comfort-accessories have not merely resulted from this change, they have played their part in creating it.

I will give you an example.

As I have stated previously, I do not do a lot of session-fishing; a 24 hour midday to midday stint being my normal choice. But earlier this season, for my first trip to a new water, I decided to extend it to 48 hours—Friday evening through to Sunday evening. On arrival, I looked around, chose my swim (perhaps a little too hurriedly because I wanted to stake my claim before other weekenders got there) and set up. In view of the fact that this was, by my standards, a long session, I had more gear than normal. It took me three trips to and from the car park to carry it all. In addition to my usual items I had a foam-mattress, food and cooking equipment, chilly-bin full of bait, water container, radio for weather forecasts, a couple of library books etc.

Within an hour of setting-up, I had a flier to the left-hand rod and landed an 18 lb mirror. I took that as confirmation that my swim choice had been a good one. A nice welcome to the new water too. I recast, but decided against putting out any more freebies in case I frightened fish that were in the area.

Darkness fell, and the night passed without further incident.

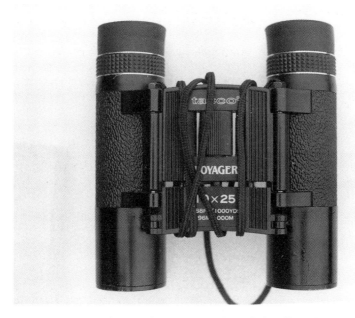

Mini-bins; useful for scanning the water—but pointless if you have so much gear
that you are disinclined to move!

The following morning dawned clear, promising a warm day. And
so it proved. It was pleasant enough laying on my bed-chair and reading
a book, but increasingly I felt that I was in the wrong spot. Yes, I had
caught a fish the previous evening, but began to suspect it had been
a stray. I kept looking up from my book and scanning the water. Then,
way down the other end of the lake, I saw a carp jump. I put down
my book and watched. In the next hour or so, I saw several more. A
move was called for. I looked at the gear that had taken so much effort
to transport to my pitch ... no way! I knew I ought to move, but could
not face the ordeal of doing so. So the rest of that day, night and the
next morning were spent as I deserved, runless.

For my usual day-only or single-night trips I carry far less gear,
and should the need arise to move, I will. Session-fishing (by my standards), and the brolly-bound inertia that accompanied it, had on that
occasion cost me fish; of that I am certain. And that is only one example;
I can recall plenty of others when I have realised I was in the wrong
swim, but could not bring myself to shift.

Do you wonder that I regard session-fishing as vastly overrated from
a tactical point of view?

I said that it had led to a change in approach. Many modern carp anglers adopt a "they'll come to us" philosophy. They bait-up heavily, then sit and wait. In general it is not a particularly effective tactic, and results in many hundreds of runless hours. It is also boring. Which is perhaps why so many carp anglers spend such a large proportion of their fishing time standing around nattering in someone else's swim, augmented by trips to the the pub or the curry house. Let us be honest, extended bivvy-bound sessions are mind-numbingly monotonous! They induce a sort of stupefying, soporific fatigue; which is why we rarely move even when we know it is necessary.

Because they spend so long in one spot, many anglers seem to think it is not important to set up quietly. I suppose they figure that no matter how noisy they are, they will be there long enough for the swim to quieten down, and for carp that have been scared off, to return.

Or don't they realise that noise scares fish?

As I write, I can remember a Sunday afternoon on Johnson's Railway Lake. Most of the weekenders had gone, and I was looking forward to a quiet afternoon and evening. I was optimistic too, because a big, warm southerly had sprung up.

I fished near the north-west bar, which was receiving the full force of the wind. Carp and tench were rolling in the waves, and I was as confident as one can be on The Railway, bearing in mind that it can be the difficult side of impossible!

About 1.30 pm I had a very fast run to a bait fished on top of ... the bar. I struck, the rod hooped over, and disaster I had a cut-off! The first time it had happened to me there.

Never mind, fish were still rolling and jumping. I was hopeful of another chance.

Then **they** arrived.

Two mountains of gear were dumped noisily on the downwind bank. I watched, first with trepidation, and then with despair, as I saw the steel-headed mallets appear. These latter-day Thors then embarked on an orgy of malleting that led me to wonder if they were tethering their bivvies with marlin-spikes.

You will be amazed to learn that following the first crashing hammer-blows, not a single fish rolled or jumped.

Don't you just love them to death!

I have said it before, and I'll go on saying it until our legislators and administrators see sense, and take the required action; the use of mallets should be a hanging offence!

Especially when I am fishing!

Most carp anglers would catch far more if they simply learned to be quiet. They would allow the rest of us to catch more, too.

I know noisy anglers and successful anglers—but I do not know

Normally I travel fairly light—so it is no great hassle to move if I find I'm in the wrong spot.

one noisy, successful angler.

Time on the bank only increases the likelihood of success if it is spent effectively; but in practice a lot of it merely compensates for bad angling.

I have met a lot of very good carp anglers, and count among my friends some of the best in UK and the continent. Some have a special flair with bait, some are technically very good, others have a very confident, single-minded attitude—but **all** have the twin talents of being able to find carp, and fish for them without scaring them.

I realise I am labouring this point, but as it is the most important element of all, I think it merits special emphasis. Not that I honestly think it will make any difference; those who cannot see that they will be more likely to succeed if they are quiet, are not likely to be influenced by my rantings. In fact, I doubt that they will be reading this section at all. They will have scanned the baits and rigs chapters, decided, "There's nothing new there," and put the book back on the shelf!

Carp come close when there is cover.

MARGIN FISHING

Margin fishing was originally taken to mean fishing with a floating crust immediately below the rod tip. Nowadays, though, it is more likely to involve the use of bottom baits, fished anywhere from the margins proper, to a gentle lob out.

Normally it works best where the banks are quiet and there is some sort of cover or sanctuary; it might be reeds, weeds, lilies, snags, overhanging trees or other vegetation.

Some margin spots are holding-areas, especially those near snags, but most are patrolling or passing places. Periodically through the day or night, individual or small groups of fish will move through and, depending on their interest and the degree of stimulus, feed as they do so.

Sometimes they just are not interested. They have a sort of earnest look about them, and a determination to get from A to B, with no distractions en route. Such fish are worth trying for though, at least you know you are in a spot where fish are, and as the day goes on their mood might change.

Others are, if not actively searching for food, willing to be tempted.

Margin weed encourages carp to come close.

A light scattering of freebies may evoke their interest, and if they like what they find, they will look for more.

I never try to create heavy feeding in this situation, because margin fish are often rather nervous, and will not stay in the pitch long enough to clear up a big bed of bait. Better, I think, to rely on a light scattering which will stimulate interest, but only take a minute or two to clear.

Particles are often effective, as are mini-boilies. A favourite approach of mine is to use small boilie-cubes, fished among a pouchful of similar freebies and a couple of pouches of particles.

It is tempting to keep peering over the edge, especially if the fish you are after are likely to be in view as they pass through. But I prefer to sit well back and not take the risk of my silhouette or shadow spooking them.

The exception to this is if I am fishing a snag-swim; but more of that later.

The sight of tackle does not seem to frighten carp, but the feel of it can. Roger Smith, who is famed for his lateral thinking, said we ought to use thick, highly visible line. Carp would then, according to Roger, see it and avoid it—and thereby not be frightened by accidently touching

I forget what this weighed; I do not even remember catching it – but I guess I must have done!

A 22lb Johnson's mirror that I caught on black-eyes.

Snaggy swims sometimes result in fish incurring slight damage during the fight –
as did this long, lean Seine common.

A 22 lb sunset mirror.

25½ lb of deep-water mirror.

it! It is an interesting idea! But I prefer to have my lines laying flat along the bottom. In calm conditions they can simply be allowed to droop, but if there is any drift it is best to use a back-lead.

I have used back-weights in one form or another for many years; in fact back in the early 70's I wrote about sliding a mud-ball attached to a nylon loop down the line. This detachable back-weight was originally used to counteract surface drag when free-lining; but I subsequently discovered that it had other advantages in that it kept the line safely below water-skiers and windsurfers, and made it look as though I was close-in fishing, even when I was not! My first non-mud back-weights were made from plastic loop earrings on which a swan-shot was pinched. These were invariably used to hold the line flat while margin fishing. This led to a curtain-hook/catherine-lead version. Now I use Richard Gardner's commercial back-leads. They are excellent.

Just a cautionary note, though; do not use back-leads where there are sharp flints or mussels on the bottom—you will suffer cut-offs if you do.

SNAG-FISHING

Occasionally we will be casting adjacent to, or between snags. A lot of pits have submerged trees and bushes that grew before it was flooded. Canals have mooring posts and bridge supports. All sorts of waters have lily and reed beds. Carp seem to be attracted to such spots; presumably it gives them a feeling of security. They can be extracted from them, but it requires modified tactics. It is not possible to allow carp to run when they pick up a bait, nor can they be allowed to run when they are hooked.

But first things first.

When casting to what are often tiny clear spots between snags, I have found that a bait-clip rig is best. The hook-link does not flail round, and is therefore much less likely to hang-up on an obstruction.

I like the rod to be angled upwards, so the tip gives me a moment's warning of a take before it registers on the alarm or indicator. The indicator must be heavy, so the line is kept as taut as possible. This is especially important if the water has any flow. The anti-backwind of the reel is engaged, and the clutch is locked.

It is necessary to sit immediately adjacent to the rods, so a take can be answered with an immediate strike.

As soon as a fish is hooked, it must be held on a tight line. This is far easier than you might imagine. With the rod held high, it absorbs every lunge, and even quite large carp can be drawn quite easily away from the danger area. The reason it works so well is because the fish

Snag-fishing on a canal. I like to angle the rods upwards, and sit right beside them.

are not given the opportunity to accelerate and gather momentum. They are being hooked whilst virtually stationary, and are therefore fighting from a standing start.

Obviously there are a few basic precautions that must be observed. In this sort of fishing, you do not wander along to the next swim for a chat; if you do, and a take occurs, you will end up with snagged fish, and probably a lost rod.

This sort of fishing places a premium on being quite because fish in such spots are resident. If they are frightened, they will not feed. Ideally casting needs to be right first time, and groundbaiting confined to a single pouchful. The fish are already there, remember, they do not need to be attracted (I doubt that groundbait achieves that, anyway). Nor do they need to be held—they are not going anywhere. A few freebies might, however, stimulate interest. A stringer obviates the need to catapult freebies out at all; but if it is necessary to cast to a really tight spot, a stringer might not be a good idea due to its possible adverse effect on accuracy.

In some snag-swims there is every likelihood that the line will rub against obstructions during the fight, and for that reason needs to be able to withstand abrasion. Wooden piles are not particularly abrasive unless they have been tarred, so 15 lb Berkley Big Game will probably suffice. But if the obstructions have rough edges, I would choose Kryston's Quick-Silver. I have not used it yet in this sort of situation, but my bench-tests convince me that it will do the job.

The rod does not need to be a brute-stick. I use an 11 ft/2¼ lb test-curve model, and find it perfect. It is not heave-and-hold fishing in the normal understanding of the term. It is more hold-and-coax, if you see what I mean. Anglers who allow fish to run into and through snags have to try to heave them out by brute-force; but the tactic I have described is altogether more refined. It is quite elegant fishing, and very importantly, does not damage fish.

I have extracted many carp in the teens of pounds, and several of twenty-plus, from snag-swims; but they pall into insignificance beside the 35 lb and 33 lb mirrors that a friend of mine saw played safely through bridge-piles and massive guide-posts.

Imagine holding those on a tight line!

OFF THE TOP

As I admitted in the bait-section, I do not do much floater fishing these days. And that is a surprise really, because water birds notwithstanding, I used to catch a high proportion of my summer carp from the surface.

I did not catch many on controller tackle, and in fact have only caught a handful in my whole carp fishing career that way, but I caught lots on freeline and tethered baits. They are the styles I know best, so it is those I shall describe. I just am not qualified to discuss the niceties of controller fishing, nor the crudities of the beach-caster rig; so I shall stick to what I know.

The most intimate style of floater fishing is stalking carp in reeds and lilies. Sometimes you see the carp themselves, but more often you see signs like shaking reed-stems or twitching lily leaves. The movements can be obvious, as if a dog were charging through them, but often will be very subtle, perhaps no more than a single broken stem describing a tiny half circle.

Obviously tackle needs to be substantial for this sort of fishing; 15 lb line, and a strong size four hook, like a Mustad 34021. The relatively heavy hook does not marry well with small pet-food floaters, so I use floater-cake, or ordinary three-day old breadcrust.

If possible the line should be hung across a convenient stem, so it does not touch the surface of the water. Sometimes, of course, the bait is being dropped into such a small gap that the line hangs more or less vertical anyway.

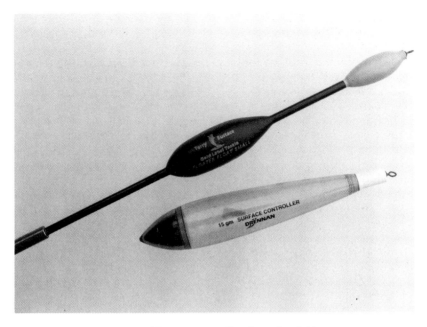

Eustace and Drennan controllers for surface fishing.

I said "dropped" quite deliberately, because often this sort of fishing is very intimate, and the bait might sometimes be within inches of the bank, occasionally actually touching marginal vegetation.

The take can be a cavalier affair, accompanied by a noisy "slurp" and an eruption of water; or it can be unbelievably gentle, as though the bait had sunk of its own volition. Either way, it is a mistake to strike too early, or fish will be missed; better to hold a foot or so of line in the free hand and strike when this is pulled taut. I usually hold the rod for this sort of fishing, although occasionally I put it on a rest, engage the anti-reverse on the reel, and hang a bottle-top bobbin, or even a pinch of dough, between a couple of rings, for bite indication. It is not a sit-back-and-relax style though; takes can come completely without warning, and too long a delay before striking will almost certainly result in a snagged carp, and possibly the rod taking a dive.

If possible the carp should be kept thrashing near the top. If it becomes immovable, there is no point continuing to heave; better to wait until the fish starts thrashing again, whereupon you can combine a heave with the carp's struggles to get it to crash its way towards you.

When nothing will shift them, friends and I have stripped down to underpants and gone in after them. Unless you are prepared to do this as a last resort, it is debatable whether such places should be fished in the first place.

Some might go further and argue that really bad snag swims should not be fished anyway; their contention being that there is too great a risk of fish being damaged. The claim has some merit, and it is undeniable that damage is more likely to occur in snag-swims than in open water. I am not entitled to moralise on this one because I have caught a great many carp in exactly the circumstances I have described, and I have to confess that a handful of those fish suffered some mouth damage as a result of the bullying I gave them. I have not used this approach for several years and, frankly, cannot visualise doing so in the future. It is a matter for individual conscience; but this much I will say—anyone who fishes in reeds or lilies, or any snag-swims for that matter, **must** use adequate tackle. No fish should ever be left trailing line, simply because the angler fished too light.

Stalking in the weeds works well in nearly every water where such swims exist; but open water surface fishing is a completely different matter, in some waters it works superbly, in others it is useless. That said, there are also waters where the carp supposedly do not take surface baits, but then someone decides to try it anyway and does well! I had an example of this on a "they don't take floater here" water where, I have to admit, my attempts to get them to show interest in free-floaters in the close-season had been a complete failure.

But one day, I was fishing bottom baits out towards an island and a bar, when I noticed some swirling over the bar. "If this was anywhere else," I thought to myself, "I'd put a floater across them."

The swirling continued. I decided I had nothing to lose, and more out of curiosity than hope, cast an anchored floater beside the bar. Literally within minutes it was away! I cannot remember the outcome, because it was a long while ago, but I think I had three takes which, due to astonishment, panic and bad angling, only resulted in one fish.

I subsequently got my act together, and in trips that followed caught a number of carp on surface baits from that water. Ironically, it is nowadays known as a good floater water, and there is usually an early season flurry when a number of fish fall to the method.

It taught me a lesson, and confirmed it was wrong to accept folklore as gospel. In the intervening years since the episode I described, I have not allowed myself to be discouraged from using floaters by a water's non-floater reputation. Often, in fairness, it has to be said that the reputation appeared justified, and the method proved to be unproductive; but just occasionally carp were more inclined to take floaters than their reputation would suggest.

Explain this if you can. I used to fish two lakes that were side by

Carp swirl at a floating crust.

side, and shared carp from the same stocking. The then fishery manager seemed to interpret his role as one of continually shunting carp from one of the club's lakes to another . . . as do a surprising number of fishery managers for some obscure reason. We will call the two lakes The Big Lake and The Small Lake; no prizes for guessing why!

The Small Lake was heavily stocked with small fish, and there came a time when it was decided to move them across into The Big Lake. Prior to their move they had been enthusiastic surface feeders, but after their move they refused to take surface baits at all.

The Small Lake was then stocked with some Redmire Commons; this being at a time when a number of Redmire Fish were sold off. Redmire, so they tell me, is a very poor floater water; but in their new home they, and their progeny (for they spawned shortly after their introduction), were suckers, both literally and metaphorically, for floaters!

There is more!

Meanwhile, back at The Big Lake, that had for years been a useless floater water, the carp suddenly became very surface-bait orientated, and lots of fish fell to the method.

Curiouser and curiouser!

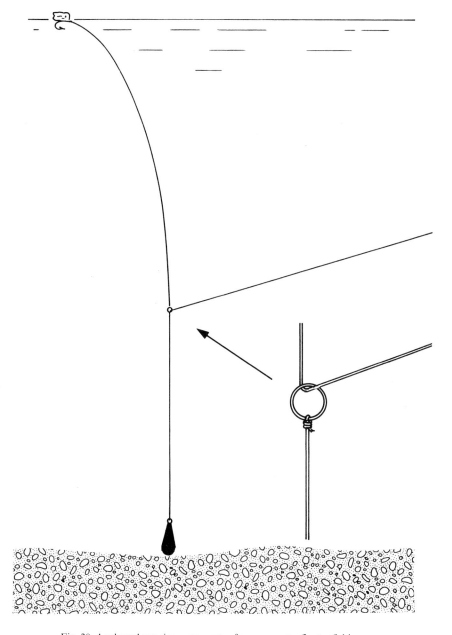

Fig. 20. Anchored running-paternoster for open-water floater fishing.

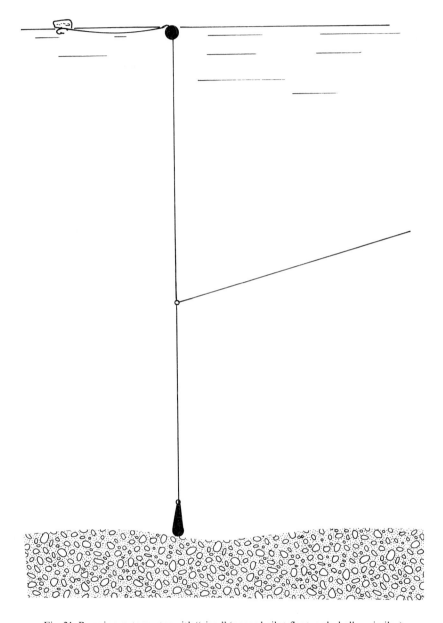

Fig. 21. Running-paternoster with "riser" (pegged pilot-float, poly-ball or similar).

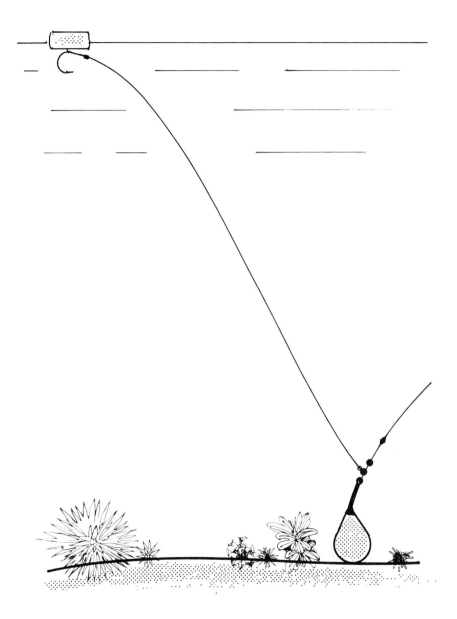

Fig. 22. Long-link floater rig.

Cloop! The crust is about to disappear down the carp's throat.

I find that sequence of events interesting, and not a little puzzling; and I would be willing to bet that it is by no means unique.

My favourite way of fishing a floating bait in open water is by means of an anchored paternoster (Fig 20). For casting the split-ring holding the lead-link is allowed to rest against the bait. After casting the bait is allowed to draw line through the split-ring until it appears on the surface. Obviously the bait needs to be fairly buoyant to manage this, so something upwards of a one inch cube of crust or floater-cake is necessary.

If, due to weed or depth of water, the bait is reluctant to come up, a larger piece of crust may be PVA'd to the floater as a buoyancy-aid. Alternatively a "riser" may be incorporated (Fig 21). It works well, but has the tendency to tangle when long-casting.

The take on this set-up is usually an exciting affair of swirls and false-passes, until all of a sudden it is engulfed either in the midst of a swirl or with a dramatic porpoise-roll! It really is exciting stuff, and as I write this I can honestly feel my pulse race as I mentally re-live some of the many, many carp I have caught this way.

When the bait disappears there is a pause, time hangs motionless for a moment, as we wait for one of two things to happen. Either the broken bait will reappear on the surface, having been spat out; or the alarm will shriek and the line will fly out!

Some days, there are more of the former, and it can be real tear-your-hair-out fishing. But often enough everything goes according to the script, and a proper take occurs.

There is, as you can imagine, a considerable angle in the line, the more so in deep water; it is therefore pointless trying to strike until the carp is pulling firmly on the end. I wait for the line to pull taut, or if the water is deep I wind down until I feel the fish; only then do I strike.

In shallow water it is possible to use very small baits such as Chum Mixers or tiny fingernail size pieces of floater-cake, by the simple expedient of using a hook-link longer than the depth of water (Fig 22). This removes the need for the bait to pull line up to the surface. It also permits the use of anchored floater in weeds, the sort of situation where even a large bait would not be able to rise.

Obviously there are physical limits to the practical length for a hook-link, and in my experience it is only really practical to use one up to the length of the rod. It is possible to go a bit beyond rod-length if the swim is a nice, open one, and the bank behind is clear of obstructions.

The delay between the disappearance of the bait and the run developing is even longer with this method than with the running-paternoster. I do not know why this should be so, but it is. So do not assume that a take has been abortive until several seconds have elapsed.

8 Hitting the Horizon

I have to smile when I look at those waters on which I first employed so-called long-range techniques—the areas to which I cast in those days would nowadays be considered middle-range at best. Those of us who developed our then concept of long-range fishing were capable of casting to what had hitherto been sanctuary areas—but the concept of the "big chuck" has changed considerably and now, in truth, there are very few UK waters where it is necessary to fish at full-stretch because there are not many out-of-reach sanctuary areas left. But that does not mean that maxi-range skills are redundant, because some of our bigger pits still require long-casting at times. And if you go abroad, many waters will be encountered that dwarf even our biggest pits. In UK, let us be honest, a 30 acre pit is a big one; but in Europe there are numerous carp waters that have their acreages measured in hundreds, and no scarcity of those that are measured in thousands.

So what I would like to do in this chapter is take a practical look at long-range fishing, and provide an update on tackle and technique. I emphasise that word "**practical**", because some of the tackle and techniques that are occasionally recommended have little relevance to real fishing situations.

The first bit of advice I would give is that it is worth developing your performance to its limit. If you can stretch your technique to enable you to cast, say, 130 yards, you will be able to cast 100 yards easily – and because you are under-performing you will be more likely to be able to do so accurately. You will be better able to cope with adverse winds too.

To achieve long distances consistently, you will need to develop good technique; although the sort of distances we require in a carp fishing context do not demand the more extreme tournament styles. They are impractical anyway, because they involve dragging terminal tackle across the ground, and require a perfectly flat bank. They are inherently inaccurate too. No one has told you that before, have they? Instead they have been content to try to impress you with talk of improbable distances and imponderable technicalities!

Out goes a long one.

So most conventional terminal-tackle-off-the-ground, over-the-head styles are quite adequate; but I recommend that you avoid techniques that involve any sort of step-through. What tends to happen is that the angler sort of topples forward as he/she (no sexist assumptions here, you see!) momentarily loses balance. It looks quite dramatic but is very inefficient. Far better to keep your feet firmly planted on the ground until after the lead has been released—that way the cast is made from a firm base, which will enhance both distance and accuracy. It is economical in terms of effort-expenditure too, and avoids casts being accompanied by gut-busting gasps and grunts which, contrary to popular assumption, do not optimise muscle-power!

A step-forward after the release of the lead, a sort of follow-through in fact, will not detract from either distance or accuracy, and is neither an advantage nor a disadvantage.

Now tackle—and first, rods. One of the unchallenged truths in distance fishing is "the longer the rod—the longer the cast". Why it is an unchallenged truth I cannot imagine, because it is absolute nonsense. I touched on this in *Big Water Carp* when I said that participants in every other sport acknowledge that the hardware has to be matched to the stature of the person using it. Thus skiers, cricketers, golfers, tennis players etc all match the size and weight of their equipment to their physical capabilities. Not so carp anglers! No matter if they are six and a half feet in their socks and weigh-in at 18 stone plus, or five feet nothing and nine stone, they will opt regardless for the sort of rod that might be ideal for the big guy, but would be an unmitigated hernia-pole for the little one. I stand 5–10 and at my lean best weigh-in at about 11½ stone (well, let's say 12 stone, and not haggle over a few inconsequential pounds!), and I find that rods of about 12 ft suit me best. Surprisingly, though, the distance advantage they give over 11 ft models is slight, only four or five yards on a full-stretch cast. Rods of 13 ft or more, I find uncomfortable and unpleasant to use—and give me no extra distance.

In my opinion, rod action is more important than length; and for long-casting I find that a fastish-taper is more effective in terms of both distance and accuracy, than slower, through-taper designs. I accept, though, that my casting style may have some bearing on my choice.

Test-curve ratings are not altogether relevant with fast and semi-fast taper designs, but they do serve to give an indication of relative stiffness. My favourite long-range rod has a test-curve of just over two and a half pounds.

The next important factor to consider is ringing. Rings have inherent penalties in that they add weight, and thus delay the recovery of the rod from its compression curve, and they provide friction, which has a "drag" effect on the line. So, we minimise those disadvantages by using as few rings as possible. When I first advocated sparse-ringing, I was told that it would result in the rod blank being unevenly loaded, or would result in rings being pulled from their whippings.

It doesn't, and they don't!

Next problem!

I was also told that the line would angle sharply across the rings, which would result in line and ring wear.

The line does angle sharply—but with modern ceramic-lined rings there are no problems with either line or ring wear.

A professional rod-maker told me that my ringing system would never be accepted, because the up-rod position of the butt ring was inconvenient for the placement of bite-indicators. It gets dafter by the moment, doesn't it?

Some anglers said that it "looked wrong", and I got unbelievably witty comments from passers-by such as, "When are you going to finish putting the rings on those rods then ...?" It is a wonder I am still in possession of intact ribs after such rapier-like wit!

Footnote: Modern blank technology and the use of higher modulus materials has led to the development of lighter, thinner rods that bring 13 ft models within the scope of those of us of average height and build.

Suffice it to say that my sparse-ringing system is now widely employed, even by those who initially rejected it as impractical. Some have even reinvented it! 'Twas ever thus.

I always used to recommend something like 8 lb test main-line in conjunction with a 20 lb shock-leader. Kevin Maddocks went further, and used 6 lb main-line (with a shock-leader) as standard for his long-range fishing; and caught carp to the mid-thirties while so doing. But times have changed, and recent years have seen our waters getting progressively weedier; with the result that we cannot afford the luxury of using light lines. Very, very rarely in summer and autumn, dare I use anything lighter than 12 lb Berkley Big Game (16 lb plus, actual).

Although I always used to recommend the use of a separate shock-leader, I now only use one when I fish with fluorescent main-line. The bulky join that is formed when the shock-leader is knotted to the main-line, results in a nasty coil-snagging protrusion that has a tendency to cause tangles. I even had a couple of Seymo tip-ring oxide inserts knocked out by leader-knots. So for the last four seasons I have been using a different system—instead of tying-in a length of thick line, I use a doubled-back portion of the main-line. The doubled-back portion is long enough to give a dozen or more turns round the reel-spool when the terminal-tackle is hanging in the correct position for casting. The line is doubled-back by means of the Bimini-Twist (20-times-around-knot), which I have described fully in both *Modern Specimen Hunting,* and *Big Water Carp.* I think it unnecessary, therefore, to explain it again here. The only advice I will give is that whereas the original description described the tying of a relatively short loop, say a couple of feet, and the loop was held apart by the knees while the knot was tied; it obviously requires a different arrangement to tie a loop of, perhaps, 20 ft. I normally use a couple of fence-posts or similar, to hold the loop open. I do not claim it is easy, because it is not—it takes practice.

By using a long-loop (or doubled-back line, whichever description you prefer) as the shock-leader, we only need one small, neat knot—and in practice I find that this does not snag coils on the reel-spool, nor does it knock out ring-inserts. So with nominal 12 lb Berkley line, I am using a shock-leader of nominal 24 lb (30 lb actual) test. Which, in view of the fact that I seldom use leads heavier than three ounces, is safe enough (a good rule-of-thumb is that you need about 10 lb of shock-leader, for every ounce of lead).

But these relatively thick lines do not make a happy marriage with normal reel-spools, the drop from the lip is too severe for really long casting. So we need to use one of the current crop of long-spool models, my choice being the Shimano Aero 4000 and the Daiwa TD2050S. Not **all** wide-spool reels are as good though—I tried another make, and found that it had a frustrating tendency to tangle in mid-cast. I do not quite know why this happened, although I suspect that it was to do with the angle of attack of the spool in relation to the butt-ring. Perhaps it would not have been a problem on rods other than mine. No difficulties with the Shimanos or Daiwas though. In conjunction with the ringing I have described, they cast smoothly and soundlessly—like the metaphorical silk in fact.

Daiwa make a **very** long spooled model called the SS3000. I understand from friends who use them that they cast fantastically, but seeing as how they weigh-in at over 20 oz, and carry a £175 price tag, they will not be to everyone's taste.

There is more to long-range fishing than the "big-chuck" of course – we have to consider the aerodynamics of terminal tackles, and how we can reconcile the sometimes conflicting requirements of long casting and effective presentation. We also need to ensure that all takes register, not just the full-blooded runs. And we want to convert as many takes as possible into safety hooked fish. There is also the problem of getting the "freebies" out to where we are casting.

Most modern terminal-rigs cast well, for the simple reason that they use relatively heavy leads; and all things being equal, a big lead will go further than a little one. But we can refine matters rather more than that crude summary might suggest.

The least aerodynamic of modern set-ups is the popular in-line lead arrangement. It is a highly efficient rig, and has the virtue that it is just about 100 per cent tangle-free when used correctly; but the lead tilts in flight due to the air resistance of the bait. That reduces the overall aerodynamics of the set-up. It is certainly good for distances up to 100 yards or so, and is my normal choice; but when I want to push the range further than that, I choose a rig that incorporates a lead mounted pendulum style (ie., hanging by one end only). A lead so mounted flies far more true than does an in-line lead, and will put an extra few yards on the cast.

The various versions of the rotary-rig also cast well; the addition of anti-tangle tube (Fig 23) ensures tangle-free flight while retaining an aerodynamic profile.

But both pendulum and "rotary" set-ups suffer from the handicap that the baited hook-link flails around in flight, and provides a considerable amount of drag. Compare the distances achieved with a lead alone, and any of the rigs described, and you will see just how much difference the baited link makes.

Some years ago some leads appeared in local tackle-shops that had a concave recess in the base. These "Darenth Leads" as they were rather naffly called (still, makes a change from every other item of carp gear being the Redmire this, or the Sayay that, doesn't it?) required the boilie to be PVA'd in the hollow recess. This supposedly increased the

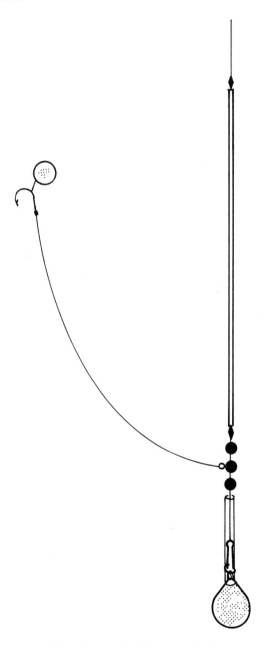

Fig. 23. Rotary rig with anti-tangle tube.

aerodynamic qualities of the tackle, and completely eliminated the flailing effect. It was one of those ideas that was good in theory, but was let down by practicalities; one being the difficulty of tying a neat PVA package that was not, in itself, bulky and air-resistant. Another problem was the impossibility of tying a PVA package round a wet lead. But the unintended characteristic of the lead that ensured its rejection, was its quaint but rather irritating habit of splattering the boilie flat if it landed on hard gravel! Not that it was much better if it landed on mud—in that instance the bait was buried!

Fortunately we can achieve the same aerodynamic effect, but without the attendant splattering and burying, by using the ubiquitous PVA to tie the bait to an up-line bait-clip. The rig is described in Chapter Two.

I am not claiming that this is the only solution, but as it is both simple and effective, I do not feel the incentive to look for anything else.

I think it is sensible to use relatively heavy indicators when fishing at long-range, because not all takes will be full-blooded runs; a proportion will be slack-liners, and heavy indicators are therefore necessary to register these as drop-backs. If you have "monkeys" equipped with a wire-loop (Micky Sly type), you can make them heavier by slipping small barrel-leads over the legs of the loop.

When fishing clutch-runner style, which I do most of the time, I use Fox Swingers rather than monkeys. Extra heavy weights are available to make these suitable for long-range registration of drop-backs, even when the line is bellied by a strong cross wind.

When a take occurs, I pick up the rod, tighten the clutch, and strike. This is where I differ from most modern carp anglers—they give a gesture-strike, more of a tug. I **strike**. I then clamp the spool with my reel-hand, and strike again. It is a full-blooded sweep-back of the rod, and I like to feel it stop short as solid contact is made.

I drop very, very few carp.

I have fished with friends who, when fishing at long-range, have dropped anything up to half of all fish hooked. On modifying their striking procedure and adopting my firm double-strike policy, their losses have virtually ceased.

I understand that some anglers might worry that this procedure is a bit brutal, and might damage fish—their concern does them credit; but this is at very long-range remember, and very little of that force is transmitted to the hook. If you doubt me, pay out 100 yards of line in a field, hold the lead in your hand, and get a friend to strike as hard as they are able. You will be surprised. (It goes without saying that you should not equip the test-tackle with a hook—yes, I know it is an obvious thing to say but, well, some people . . .).

Footnote: Please ensure that the shock-leader knot will pass through all terminal tackle components; otherwise a carp that breaks the line might be condemned to tow a lead.

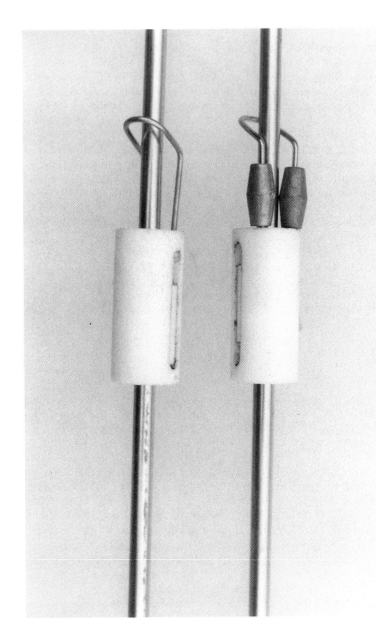

"Monkeys"—unweighted and weighted versions.

Modern tackle is so good for distance casting, that one of the main difficulties associated with long-range work is getting "freebies" out to the fishing area. Sometimes, of course, it can be achieved by casting from one place, and putting the bait out from another—like those situations where the casting is done to a bank from which fishing is not allowed, or is impractical, but it is possible and permissible to gain access for putting out baits. But that sort of situation is by no means commonplace, and more often we are faced with a fishing area that is, quite simply, very difficult to reach with "freebies".

Where it is allowed, and will not annoy other anglers, an inflatable dinghy is useful—but as with so many facilities, this sort of thing tends to get abused. I fish waters where some selfish individuals are forever paddling about and playing pond-admiral. Inflatables should only be used when there are no other anglers on the water—or they are far enough away to make it unlikely that they will be disturbed.

Then there are those little remote-control motorised boats that will deliver a batch of baits to the chosen spot. I have never used one of these, and doubt if I ever will; but I do not share the indignation of those who regard them as in some way "unsporting". I just think they are inappropriate, and would object strongly to sharing a water with anglers who regularly created a disturbance by playing with the damn things. But if someone is alone on a water, and wants to use one, I cannot see the objection. Mind you—I don't understand why they don't simply sell their fishing gear, and join a model-boat club, or go train-spotting or something . . .

And who wants to lug a toy boat round the far side of a big pit? The Lego takes up quite enough space as it is . . .!

The most practical methods are a wrist-rocket type catapult or, even better once you get the hang of it, a Cobra throwing-stick.

When I use a catapult, I always wear a leather gardening-glove on my catapult-hand, this to prevent my knuckles being reduced to a bruised and bloody pulsating mass. Why so few anglers use gloves for protection, I do not understand—unless it is some perverse macho-thing, "I can take it," and all that.

Not that throwing-sticks are without their problems—they lead to throwing-stick-elbow. This is painful, and steadfastly refuses to go all the time you continue to use one. Which means you will only be free of pain in the close-season! But as soon as you start pre-season pre-baiting, it returns as bad as ever . . .

The best method I have used, in terms of both distance and accuracy, is to employ a spare rod to put out what is, in effect, a stringer.

I use a rod that will handle a heavier lead than the one I am using on my baited tackles. It can be rigged with lighter main-line too, because it does not have to land carp.

The lead is attached to the end of a heavy shock-leader by means of a large, strong link-swivel.

To the link-swivel I attach a mono-loop of sufficient length to accommodate between three and five boilies (depending on their size). Large-ish holes are made through each boilie, and they are slid on the loop. The loop is pulled through a split-ring that is tied-in a few inches above the lead. A tiny roll of PVA or half a Disprin tablet is tucked in the loop to act as a stop and keep the boilies in place (Fig 24). The rig is cast to the required spot, and left for a few seconds for the PVA/Disprin to dissolve. The baits are then released from the "stringer" with a sharp, false-strike.

The set-up casts well because it is aerodynamic, and because the "stringer" cannot flail around in flight. This is, in fact, a slightly modified version of something I described years ago, when I wrote a weekly feature in *Anglers Mail*. I called it the "necklace" system of groundbaiting—but to my surprise, the idea never really caught on.

Subsequently, and in a slightly different form, the principle re-emerged and achieved widespread popularity. It was re-christened too, and the name "stringer" is the one that stuck.

But whatever its origins, it works extremely well. It is **far** more accurate than either a catapult or a throwing-stick, and has the added advantage that it completely beats bait-intercepting gulls. It does not beat tufted-ducks, but then nothing does. Well, that is not quite true. Two of the waters I fish are shared by shooting syndicates . . .!

By varying the weight of the lead, and the number of baits on the necklace/stringer, you can ensure that the baiting-rod casts exactly the same distance as the rod-proper. There is no need for markers, and no need to gauge range. Once distances have been synchronised, you just whack it out as far as possible, and it goes to the exact spot every time.

It is not, however, suitable for mass-baiting. I would not, for example, want to cast more than four or five times, for fear of being more likely to scare carp than encourage feeding.

One final aid to long-range baiting and casting that is worth mentioning, is a pair of chest-waders. Some big waters, particularly French barrages in non-mountainous regions, have very wide, shallow margins. Chest-waders will enable an extra 30 yards or so to be added to the cast.

By its nature, long range fishing is done on big waters—and big waters often have to be shared with other water users. In UK that usually means wind-surfers, and occasionally dinghy sailors. These vary in their nuisance-quotient, depending on their level of expertise. The less experienced they are, the more likely they are to "lose it". Because we often fish the down-wind end of a water, and when wind-surfers "lose it", they end up there too—we tend to find ourselves being reluctant bedfellows. And understandably, tempers can get a bit frayed.

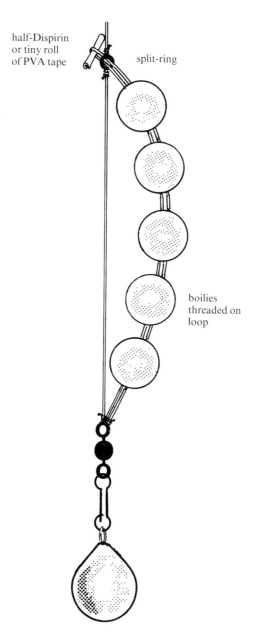

Fig. 24. Stringer-loop long-range baiting.

There is no real solution. Back-leads, where their use is practical, keep the line below keel-boards. But when beached wind-surfers come ashore and paddle along the margins to find a more suitable take-off point, they render fishing untenable. Which is a pity, because I do not think that carp are at all worried by their activities, and continue feeding regardless. Certainly I have caught carp from disturbed areas; including one memorable occasion when I plucked one from beneath a beginners' class, despite their constant falling-in and the whipping of the water to a frenzied froth!

At least you can see wind-surfers. Not so divers. On two occasions, one in UK and once on the continent, I have hooked scuba-divers! They fought well too. I could not hold them on 12 lb line!

I do not think these scare carp either. I remember one occasion when I watched the progress of two divers by their bubble-trails. Bubbles burst alongside my marker-float, so close that I expected to see it dragged under. Within a minute or two of their having passed by, I had a run and hooked a very powerful fish. It subsequently turned out to be a 24½ lb mirror. Which was both a relief and a surprise, because initially I thought I might have hooked one of the divers.

In France, a lot of waters are designated as Plan d'eau (freshwater leisure areas), on which there will be all the activities so far mentioned, plus swimmers, kiddies in inflatables, paddlers, sun-bathers ... although the last-named group is not without its compensations. If I have no choice but to share a carp water with others, I will settle for bikini-clad nubilia.

9 Deep Waters

Increasingly these days I seem to be fishing deep waters. One of the most important lessons I have learned is that it is not enough to locate carp laterally, as it were; it is also necessary to locate them in a vertical plane. It is possible to be in the right swim, but unless the baits are presented at precisely the right depth, no takes will occur.

Before proceeding further, I think it might be helpful if I give an actual example to illustrate my point. A couple of years ago, at the back end of winter, I fished a Benelux gravel pit of about 30 acres. The margins sloped gently at first, but approximately 50 yards out there was a sort of convex shelf, beyond which the bottom dropped away fairly rapidly to a maximum depth of 31 feet.

I thought it unlikely that carp would feed just anywhere on the shelf, so I decided to place my baits in three carefully located, pre-measured depths. These positions were ascertained by means of a depth-testing/marker-float on a spare rod.

The left hand rod was cast to 15 feet, the middle rod to 18 feet and the third rod to 21 feet (Fig 25). I emphasise that these positions were very accurately measured; my preferred method being to cast a running marker-float (Fig 26), and pay out line in yard-long pulls until the float appears on the surface. If the depth is too great, indicating that I have cast too far, I wind the float down, retrieve a little way, and try again. When I have found the precise depth I am seeking, I use the float as a marker to which I cast, and as a target for my freebies.

This was done for all three rods.

If a run occurred I could duplicate the bait position exactly on subsequent casts; this would be impossible if test-depth fishing was done in a random or imprecise way.

A run did occur. It came at about 2.30 pm, to the rod that had been cast to 21 feet. The fight was a real heart-in-the-mouth affair because I could feel the line rubbing on the shelf as the fish bored down to the deeper water beyond. On being brought up over the shelf, it set off on a long, kiting run to my right. I was tremendously relieved when it eventually wallowed over the net. It weighed 25½ lb, and was my first from

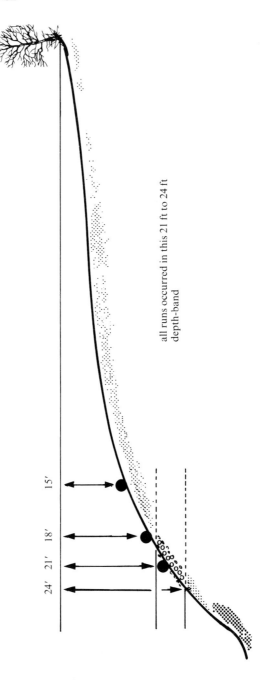

all runs occurred in this 21 ft to 24 ft
depth-band

24' 21' 18' 15'

Fig. 25. Test-depth fishing to ascertain feeding-depth.

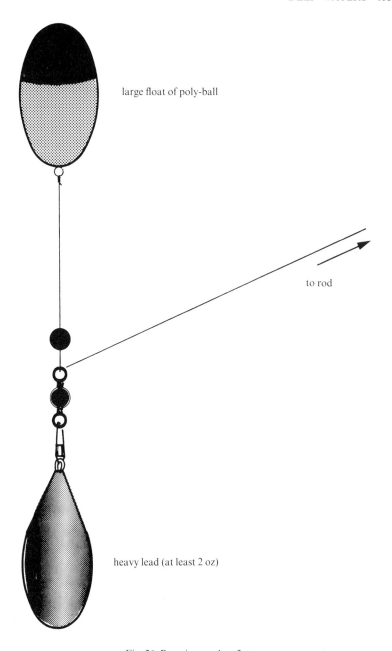

large float of poly-ball

to rod

heavy lead (at least 2 oz)

Fig. 26. Running marker-float.

the water. It was almost certainly the first time the fish had ever been caught too, because the water is hardly fished on account of being rated "very difficult" by those who know it. Further evidence of the fish's probable "virgin" status was provided by the fact that the veil on the roof of its mouth was still intact.

Veil?

Uncaught carp have what Mike Wilson described as a "curtain", and I call a "veil", hanging down from the roof of the mouth, just behind the section that extends and telescopes. It comprises very delicate, membraneous tissue that, I imagine, is part of a carp's natural feeding equipment. I suspect it traps tiny food items, larvae and the like, during suck-blow feeding. Most anglers have never seen this veil, most are not even aware that uncaught carp have one—hardly surprising when we realise that on many waters it is considered quite an event to catch a carp that even has its face intact!

Because of the sort of fishing I do, a high proportion of the fish I catch have this veil. I have no interest in the sort of carp fishing where it is otherwise.

Anyway, back to my deep water. Not surprisingly I recast to the same spot. I decided to leave the 18 feet rod where it was; but relocated the 15 feed rod to 24 feet. I thus "sandwiched" the successful rod between one a little deeper, and one a little shallower. I wanted to establish if 21 feet was the optimum feeding depth, or the upper or lower limit of feeding.

No further runs occurred that day, nor the next; so no more information was immediately forthcoming. But the following day, in an unpromising north-easterly after an early morning frost, a very fast run to the 24 feet rod produced another mid-twenty.

I had now taken fish at 21 feet and 24 feet. A pattern was beginning to emerge.

I kept those rods where they were, but relocated the 18 feet rod at 27 feet. And there, really, the story ends. The 27 feel rod merely succeeded in producing roach (some big ones too, Geordie Mike took one of about two pounds). Subsequent carp, topped by one of just under 27 lb (that had a veil, too), all fell within the 21 to 24 feet depth-band.

In the example I have quoted I was able to use three rods, and there is no denying that in this sort of situation it certainly helps to be able to do so. Actually I was subsequently informed by the bailiff that only two rods were permitted; but fortunately my genuinely innocent transgression had, by then, enabled me to ascertain the feeding depth.

Two rods certainly slow down the process and, in truth, the restriction makes the identification of the critical depth a bit more difficult, in that you cannot "sandwich" the successful rod in the way I have described. But the basic trial-and-error approach still applies, and is still viable.

Mike puts a bait out to very deep water on a frosty morning.

As I write it is late December, and for the last two months I have spent a day a week on a 50-odd acre pit that has a maximum depth of 52 feet. When I started fishing there at the tail end of October, the fish were in the 25 feet region; but since then they have gradually dropped to deeper water, and my most recent captures have been from the 31 feet to 36 feet range. In truth the fishing has been quite easy, and I have averaged a couple of fish a day; but apart from those I have caught, very few have been taken. It is quite a hard-fished water, but most of the anglers who fish there are reluctant to cast much beyond the margins (it is about 12 feet deep only a rod-length out), and regard the deep water beyond as a sort of no-go area.

They are not untypical; most carp anglers seem to have a bit of a hang-up about fishing deep water, presumably because they regard carp as shallow water fish. I can understand that someone who has only caught them from relatively shallow water might find it difficult to believe that they are willing and able to feed in the deeps; but restricting fishing to shallow areas will prove to be a very serious handicap.

My recent captures from depths up to 36 feet are the deepest at which I have caught carp; but the circumstance is not unique because

No monster, 15 lb actually, but notable in that it came from 36 feet—the deepest
water from which I have caught carp.

several years ago I caught them in a reservoir at about 35 feet, and I
have caught lots in depths of 20 feet plus.

I have no doubts that in the right circumstances carp will feed in
deeper water still; Rod Hutchinson told me he caught fish from Cassein
at something like 90 feet! Now that **is** deep! I do not have any sort of
mental-block about deep water; but I have to confess that 90 feet would
stretch my confidence to its limit . . . and then some!

Why do carp go deep; and having done so, why do they feed within
such a narrow depth-band? I do not pretend to know the answer to that
one; but I have come to a few conclusions.

Temperature is undoubtedly an important factor, especially in summer; but I do not think it provides a neat rule-of-thumb by which we
can predict feeding depth. It does not work like that. I recall catching
a lot of summer margin feeders from very shallow water in a heatwave.
With the change to cool weather, the carp did not conveniently slip down
the slope to deeper water, and continue to feed. They very inconveniently
decided to disappear altogether; leaving me to try to relocate them. Which
I failed to do!

So although I think it likely that there is a vertical movement in response to temperature (shallower as water warms, deeper as it cools), it is by no means an invariable or even a particularly predictable response.

What tends to happen is that once a feeding depth is identified, it remains fairly constant despite changes in weather and its influence on water temperature. This is particularly the case when fishing deep (say, 20 feet plus). My experience suggests that whereas a bitterly cold north-easterly may inhibit feeding, and a lovely, mellow south-westerly may encourage it; if it occurs at all, it will fall within the identified feeding band, and will not relocate itself up or down the slope.

Water pressure is doubtless a factor too. I recall fishing an estate lake for pike many years ago, and it became obvious that they responded to the changing water levels that occurred when the outflow was operated. This in response to the lake's feeder stream showing signs of spate. They moved towards the dam end of the lake when the level dropped, and towards the inlet-end when it rose; presumably to keep a constant depth over their heads. It was, I suspect, a comfort response. I think those pike adjusted their position, rather than adjust their pressure equilibrium mechanism.

I think this applies to carp as well as to pike; but I have no real evidence to support my belief, so I leave you to give as much credence to the idea as you think it deserves.

The nature of the bottom is another, and much more predictable factor. That 21 feet to 24 feet feeding area that I referred to in my original example, consisted of a hard, stony bottom. This was easily felt as the tackle was retrieved; and the lead showed ample evidence in the form of dents and abrasions. Beyond the 25 feet mark, it was much less stony, although it was still quite firm; but beyond 27 feet it was silty, and baits left there for any length of time acquired a horrible silty smell.

I was not at all surprised to find that the stony area was the place to be.

Dissolved oxygen must come into the reckoning too; although it is unlikely that this will play as important a role in winter as in summer. Cold water usually has a high oxygen level, and this at a time when a carp's oxygen requirement is at its lowest.

Natural food supplies such as shrimp, mussels, snails and various larvae, have their preferences/requirements with regard to where they live; and no carp is going to get much of a living unless it feeds where food supplies are most abundant.

So what I think we end up with is a depth-band in which the combination of water temperature, water pressure, dissolved oxygen and available food, combine to produce a sort of "comfort-zone". And in deep water this zone remains fairly constant, unless a significant and prolonged weather change alters it.

In many deep waters carp are very reluctant to show, but that is not to say that they never do so; sometimes they will roll and leap just as they do in shallower waters. But here is a strange thing; when they show over deep water, it usually accompanies or precedes feeding, even though the bottom may be 30-odd feet below. I find all jumping and rolling a puzzling phenomenon, but never more so than when it accompanies deep water feeding.

Brian Mills mentioned to me that when carp are hooked in deep water, they discharge a lot of gas as they are forced to ascend the marginal slope. He is right; but I had not noticed it until he pointed it out. When we discussed it while fishing together one day, he suggested that it might be a pressure adjustment. I think he is probably correct. That led him to speculate that deep water rolling might be for the express purpose of taking-in air to counter the effects of pressure, prior to deep water feeding. The gas-discharge situation in reverse, in fact.

It is an interesting idea; perhaps someone who understands the mechanism of pressure-adjustment in fish might be able to comment?

So let me try to summarise.

In summer, especially if the weather is warm and the water temperature quite high, there will often be a tendency to move to shallow areas such as the margins, bars and plateaux.

As temperatures fall in autumn, there will probably be a tendency to leave the shallows and gradually move down to deeper water.

As temperatures drop further, so the carp will position themselves in quite a narrow "comfort-zone", and they will stay there unless the weather changes very significantly.

With the onset of winter proper (night frosts, daytime temperatures in low single figures Centigrade etc) the "comfort-zone" will get progressively deeper.

If the weather becomes substantially milder towards the back-end of the season, the "comfort-zone" might revert to autumn levels. It is likely to remain thus until well after Easter because big, deep waters warm up very, very slowly. This is worth bearing in mind if you make a trip to the continent in the UK close-season. Further to that; if late May/early June results in a heatwave, which it often does, margin areas will warm up rapidly, and carp will move up in large numbers.

As an addendum to the foregoing, I ought to mention that it is not unusual for some carp to move to the margins after dark—this can happen even in the middle of winter. So if fishing a deep water at night, I think it is worth casting one rod short, for a trial period anyway, just in case this occurs.

Thus far I have assumed that there is some sort of marginal slope. This is not always the case. In north Kent we have a number of chalk-pits; and these have sheer sides because chalk is quarried, rather than dug. I have only fished one chalk pit, and that was more than 15 years ago.

A 20lb mirror that accompanied another just under 20lb, two or three 7lb plus
tench and a wasp-sting!

A beautiful sunrise – and a big carp is hooked. What a way to start the day!

Mike bends into one – but neither of us can remember what it weighed.

A 26½lb near-leather taken beneath a brooding sky and photographed by flash.

Sheer-sided chalk-pit. Such waters have no marginal shallows to speak of.

It had an average depth of from 30 to 40 feet. There were no marginal shallows at all; the only areas that qualified as semi-shallow being a ramp that once carried lorries down to the bowels of the quarry, and a flooded road.

I confined my fishing to early summer, and caught my carp from the top. Some caught fish on bottom baits on the ramp and road—but few bothered to try the deep areas because of the "carp don't feed in the deeps" belief, which was even more entrenched then than it is now. In winter, on the other hand, carp were caught from the deeps. In fact, some anglers considered it a better winter than summer water.

Those who fish overseas in mountainous areas will find sheer-sided lakes too; only more so in that depths are likely to be considerably greater than in chalk-pits.

I have never fished such waters, so am not qualified to comment; but articles I have read by those who have been to Grand Canaria, suggest that whereas there are areas of sheer rock plummeting vertically down to vast depths, there are also natural bays and similar, where much shallower water can be found.

As UK anglers go further afield and fish lakes in alpine regions, so information regarding carp behaviour in these immensely deep waters will emerge. I have no doubts that it will prove worthwhile, because some very large carp have already been taken in Austria and Switzerland, despite very little serious carp fishing being done. Definitely one for the Marco Polos in our midst.

One final observation that might be worth bearing in mind, is that carp sometimes hover at mid-depth over very deep water. Andy Little has written of how on Cassein he picked up big-fish signals on an echo-sounder at about 40 feet; this in 90 feet of water. Others have quoted similar examples, on lakes other than Cassein too. It seems improbable that this has anything to do with food supplies, and is, I am sure, an example of carp finding the aforementioned comfort-zone.

I would doubt the worth of trying to fish for them at mid-water, and certainly would not expect any amount of bait to succeed in "pulling them down" to the bottom. I have read that higher than usual levels of amino-acid attractors may succeed in doing this. I think the belief is erroneous; and is yet another example of anglers placing far too much reliance on bait.

Were I to encounter this situation, I would look for an area where the depth of water duplicated that at which those hovering fish were located. If, for example, I found them at 40 feet, in 90 feet of water; I would select somewhere where the depth was 40 feet. I cannot quote an example of this having been successful for me, because I have never used an echo-sounder as a fish-locator; when I have used one it has been purely as an electronic "plummet" to ascertain depth, bottom make-up, weeds etc. But I am confident it would be more successful than trying to pull them down with amino-attractors.

It seems to be a characteristic of carp caught from deep water that they fight very hard. Partly this is due to the fact that they rarely embark on the reel-screeching runs of those hooked in shallower water, so they tire less quickly. But I suspect that it is also a reaction to the discomfort of pressure change. Carp can certainly adjust to the change, but I prefer to play safe and release mine immediately after capture; only sacking them for sufficient time to set up the camera.

10 The Weed Problem

No angler can fail to have realised that there has been an incredible increase in the extent and density of weed in many of our waters. It was not so many years ago that the gravel-pits on which I spend most of my fishing time were fairly barren waters—even mature pits tended to be relatively weed-free. Now the majority of those waters are densely weeded for most of the summer and autumn—it is thick weed too, real pull-for-a-break stuff.

Why has it happened?

A popular view is that recent mild winters are responsible; and it is a tempting theory because the exceedingly mild winters of 1988/89 and 1989/90 certainly saw relatively little reduction in the extent of the weed. I even saw new weed-growth in January, which is a pretty bizarre state of affairs in anyone's book! But mild winters are not, in my opinion, a particularly significant element in the equation—after all, if they were, then continental waters would be similarly affected would they not? They have had mild winters too. But such is not the case. The gravel-pits I fish in northern Europe are beautifully weed-free, just as ours used to be.

I think there are two main reasons for the change—they are independent yet, at the same time, inter-related.

The first factor is a radical change in the sort of weed that we are finding in our waters. Nearly every pit I fish is infested with Canadian pondweed (Elodea canadensis). The trouble with Elodea is that it spreads in an alarming and quite unrestrained manner. It is exceedingly tough and can survive all through the year—although in shallow water, and conditions of very low winter temperatures and high winds, will get "chopped up" and deposited on the downwind bank. Not that this is necessarily a good thing, because those broken fragments can take root and grow into new plants.

Elodea was introduced from North America in about 1840, and according to John Clegg (*Pond Life*, Frederick Warne and Co Ltd, 1956), quickly became so rampant as to be a pest. After which, so Clegg tells us, it became less abundant. Since then it has obviously had a resurgence, and has reached pest proportions again.

Why, after behaving itself for so long, has it suddenly "exploded"?

The answer to which, brings me to the second factor—and this is one I have written about before. In parts of the UK we suffer from alarmingly high levels of nutrients in underground water supplies, and this leads to eutrophication (over fertilisation) of pits and lakes fed by the affected ground-water.

The reasons for the excessive levels of nutrients are undoubtedly rather complex; but despite their frequent indignant disclaimers, there is absolutely no doubt in my mind that farmers qualify for a considerable proportion of the blame. The excessive use of fertilisers, hitherto encouraged by EEC agricultural policy, has led to contamination of the ground-water with nitrates. This, combined with historically high levels of dissolved phosphates that have got into the ground-water via river systems (due to our less than savoury practice of dumping sewage in them), creates perfect circumstances for weed growth. Or to be more accurate, excessive weed growth.

Unfortunately, as tends to be the way with ecological opportunism, the toughest and least desirable weeds, chief among them being Elodea, profited most from the nutrient bonanza. That is what I meant when I said that the two factors, although independent, were also inter-related.

The bad news is that the situation is here to stay—and will probably get worse. The even worse news is, waters that have currently escaped being overrun by weed in general, and Elodea in particular, will doubtless become affected before very long. A pessimistic view? No, just a realistic one.

Even if local councils stopped dumping sewage in rivers, and farmers stopped putting excessive amounts of fertiliser on the land (changes in EEC agricultural policy are afoot which might result in that desirable state of affairs), the existing accumulation of contaminants is so extensive that it will be very many years before available nutrients are used up, and the situation starts to improve. There are, as politicians are so fond of saying when confronted with long-term problems of their own making, "No quick-fix solutions."

So we are stuck with the problem—unless of course the eutrophication leads to the development of algal blooms which, by increasing the turbidity of the water, cause all sub-surface weed to die.

This lowers dissolved oxygen levels to such an extent that fish deaths can occur. If fish survive, the fishing will be very poor—after all, your appetite would hardly be enhanced by living in a state of near anoxia, would it? The dead weed then produces a thick layer of foul smelling ooze which, being rich in nutrients, results in the weed being worse than ever when it becomes re-established!

Johnson's Railway Lake, where an algal bloom killed all the weed in 1990 and covered the bottom with foul, black ooze.

So we have to either learn to live with it, or deal with it.

Physical weed-removal, by cutting or dragging, is a possibility, but is ineffective in that it is always a short-term solution. I worry too that it has a drastic effect on the water's eco-system in that large quantities of natural food forms (snails, larvae etc) are removed along with the weed.

Then there is the use of chemical weed-killer. I have seen this done well, and seen it done disastrously. In the hands of experienced operatives it can be effective, and it is no doubt safe, but I have an instinctive aversion to the use of alien chemicals in a fishery. It smacks too much of husbandry and takes away the natural, wild feel of a water. It is altogether too artificial. The dead weed forms the aforementioned stinking black ooze too, which can exacerbate the weed problem in future years. And if weed-killer is used by well-meaning but inexpert operatives, there are obvious dangers to the eco-system, the fish, and no doubt, the operatives themselves.

I reckon chemicals should be seen as a very last resort—and when that last resort is deemed to have arrived, they should **only** be used by, or under the supervision of, a trained and qualified operative.

Ken Crow with his one-time record grass-carp of 16 lb. It actually weighed 16 lb 10 oz (I witnessed it), but Ken mistakenly claimed the lower weight.

So if we cannot pull it out, and cannot kill the stuff with chemicals, presumably we have to learn to live with it. Probably we will—which is unfortunate, because those of us who fish affected waters know that by mid-July, or thereabouts, they can become virtually unfishable. But there **is** a simple solution. And it is one that benefits us as anglers, yet poses no threat to the eco-system. All we need do, is introduce grass-carp. The white amur, as it is usually called in Europe, is a very efficient weed-cropper. As an example, consider Ken Crow's Honeycroft fishery. It contains just enough grass-carp to keep the weed situation under control; with the result that the lake holds grass-carp of record breaking size, yet only holds weed in beneficial quantities. At one time this particular lake had an horrendous weed problem, but good management via the introduction of grass-carp solved it.

Those who worry that grass-carp might adversely affect the welfare and growth of other species would certainly have their fears allayed if they fished Honeycroft, because the mirrors and commons have a growth-rate that ranks among the fastest I have ever encountered. There are spectacular stocks of other species too.

I have also encountered grass-carp in France. A couple of years ago I fished a ballast-pit in the middle Loire region, which is kept virtually weed-free by a stocking of approximately 10 grass-carp to the acre. There are big grass-carp in the water, and big mirrors and commons too.

So what is the problem?

If anglers benefit, grass-carp benefit, and other species are certainly not handicapped in any way—where are the debits?

There are no debits as such; but there are difficulties. If you telephone fish-suppliers and enquire about purchasing grass-carp, you will encounter difficulty number one—there are none to be had.

In the unlikely event of your being able to locate supplies of grass-carp, your next move would be to contact the NRA Fisheries Department to seek permission to introduce them, and you will encounter problem number two—they are unlikely to allow you to do so.

Which, considering that they seem to be a perfect answer to what will undoubtedly become a progressively worse problem, is a bit of a shame is it not?

So—NAC (who?), NFA and NRA (Fisheries Dept) ... over to you. What chance is there that you will get round to addressing what is set to become a major and accelerating problem? But it need not be, because the solution is so simple.

I can perfectly well understand sensible caution with regard to the risk of spreading disease. I have seen the effects of SVC, for example, with my own eyes, so would not support stocking with any fish that were not certificated disease-free. But that is not the reason for the lack of official support for grass-carp. The trouble is that we are still suffering from the misguided and inappropriate blaming of all East Anglian fishery problems on the poor old zander. Fishery officers are worried that if they sanction grass-carp stockings, they will lay themselves open to being held responsible for subsequent disasters, even if they are unrelated to the introductions. I can sympathise with their point of view—in the afore-mentioned East Anglian fiasco, zander only narrowly escaped being blamed for the demise of the North Sea herring-fleet, and local incidents of sheep-worrying!

So, although the weed problem could be mitigated by the introduction of grass-carp; I, for one, will not hold my breath!

In the event of circumstances changing, and grass-carp becoming available, may I make a plea that a **total and complete** ban on their retention be introduced. That includes carp-sacks and keepnets. Grass-carp do not cope well with retention, they soon become distressed and, if not released immediately, will die.

A few years ago the Military Canal in Kent was stocked with small grass-carp, but brain-dead fools put them in keepnets, and guess what ...? You will be astonished to learn that the Military Canal no longer contains grass-carp!

So it still has a weed problem—and doubtless those who put grass-carp in keepnets are among those who are grizzling loudest.

As well as the types of weed that last all through summer and autumn, there are others than have a much shorter season. A syndicate water I fish in Essex has an extremely tough, branched, grassy sort of weed (I have not been able to identify it) that renders many areas practically unfishable for the first few weeks of the season. But come August, and it starts to break away and form large, floating rafts. By the end of the month, the water is virtually weed-free! I have encountered a similar phenomenon, but with a completely different variety of weed, on one of the Kent lakes I sometimes fish. The solution to the weed problem on those waters is, quite simply, patience.

Yet another annual development in nutrient-rich waters is algae. There are innumerable varieties, and they are all horrible! One sort creates a sort of green-paint scum along the windward margin. Another type looks like squillions of individual strands of cotton-wool, and it makes the underwater length of line look like thick hairy string. Very disconcerting! It is even worse when retrieved, and forms great, oily, hanging globs. When it dries it makes the line feel stiff and rough. It is awful stuff! I have **never** done well when a water has been badly affected by any sort of algae, so I have given up trying, and now simply fish elsewhere.

COPING WITH IT

If the problem will not go away, we have to cope with it. The first essential is to use sensible tackle. "Sensible" means heavy enough to land every fish hooked. It annoys me intensely when I hear about anglers losing fish after fish due to line breakages in weed. What is the matter with these people? It is understandable if the severity of the weed problem is under estimated, and a fish might become immovably snagged and subsequently lost. But to let it happen again, and again, and again ... It is incomprehensible unless, of course, the angler concerned has suffered a complete neural shutdown, or has been taking Stupid Pills.

Not only does inadequate tackle lead to lost fish, and snap-offs; but those lengths of broken line form a weed-bound cat's cradle of mono that can make it almost impossible to land fish, even when sensible tackle **is** used. Snagged underwater mono results in yet more carp becoming immovably snagged, and will cut through line while fish are being played.

So sensible tackle **must** be used.

When a hooked fish beds-down in weed, there are two tactics that will usually get it out. The first is the steady pull. After a while this is often answered by the carp "kicking" back, whereupon, if all goes well, it will fight its own way clear.

One extracted from the weed.

The second method is to slacken off, put the rod in the rests, and wait. More often than not, a carp will get its "second-wind" then swim out of the weedbed. Carp are quite cooperative in this respect and, paradoxically, are easier to extract from weed than are pike or tench of only a quarter their size. You will grow old waiting for those to swim out of weeds, but carp generally make a move within five to ten minutes.

If neither of those approaches work we have to resort to the pull-for-a-break technique which, in essence, means that we pull harder and harder, until something gives. It should **not** be the line. Hopefully we will manage to dislodge or uproot the clump of weed in which the carp has buried itself, and can then go on to land the fish. Or perhaps the hook will straighten, in which case we lose the fish, but do not condemn it to trail a broken line; nor do we knit the weeds with a non-degradable length of the stuff.

There comes a point, of course, when we have to ask ourselves if we can justify fishing really heavily weeded areas in the first place. When the severity of the weeds is such that we have to resort to pulling-for-a-

Footnote: **Never** pull-for-a-break by bending the rod past its intended curve, or it may splinter—instead point the rod at the fish/snag/weeds and pull with it held straight.

break with every fish hooked, with the consequent risk of causing mouth-damage, then maybe we should leave such spots alone. Trouble is, if we quit fishing mega-weed swims, someone else will do so, and will possibly be the sort who fishes too light and leaves them tethered, or trailing long lengths of snapped mono ... So by leaving heavily weeded swims alone, we might unwittingly do the carp a disservice.

It is a dilemma. I suppose it ultimately boils down to a conscience thing; we may not be able to prevent carp being abused, but we can ensure that we are not personally responsible.

An afterthought. We cannot prevent carp burying themselves in weed, but we can mitigate the problem by hitting runs as quickly as possible. Many anglers are terribly irresponsible in this respect, including some who should know better. I live near the Johnsons group of lakes, one of which is the well known Railway Lake, which until a couple of years ago was very weedy (blue-green algae made the water so turbid that weed could not photosynthesise, so it died). At best the fishing on the Railway Lake is slow; which results in anglers wandering round for a chat to their friends. Many times I have seen a group gathered in someone's pitch, while their rods were left unattended. I am not talking next-swim-unattended, but round-the-other-side-of-the-lake-unattended. It is inexcusable.

Brother Martin wrote a letter to one of the magazines criticising this sort of behaviour, which elicited replies from a couple of well-known anglers who accused him of being holier-than-thou, and begrudging people enjoying themselves.

They are wrong of course. Neither Martin nor I object to people enjoying themselves. We enjoy ourselves when we go fishing, but hopefully not at the expense of the fish, and not in a way that disturbs other anglers. But their concept of enjoyment is more appropriate to Benidorm or Blackpool, than the banks of a carp lake.

PRESENTATION

Bait presentation is difficult in weedy swims, and modern methods exacerbate the situation. The heavy lead plummets through the weed, resulting in the whole end-tackle, bait included, being buried from sight.

Where the weed is not too severe, and I think there is a chance of a bottom-bait being found, I do not mind the bait being dragged through it. But I encase the hook in PVA tape to ensure that it does not hang-up on a weed-stem on the way down. Where weed is very bad, such a limited measure is not much help.

If weed forms a canopy, it can be much more sparse down below than it appears to be when viewed from the surface. Kevin Maddocks caught the then record Ashlea carp by tying the bait to a heavy lead with PVA tape, and blasting this through the canopy to the clearer water below. Kevin even tied his freebies to stones, again with PVA, to get them through the weed.

By choice, though, I will try to find clear spots, and these can usually be found even in the weediest water. If they are small, as they often are, they can only be hit with any accuracy at close-range; which is fine if carp come close, but of limited usefulness if they do not!

If there are not any suitable clear spots, or they are too small and too far from the bank to make hitting them a viable proposition, I think it is best to enclose the hook inside the bait, and dispense with the lead altogether.

Now, there is a revolutionary concept!

What shall I call it? I know, I will call it "free-lining"!

Most carp anglers have relegated free-lining to the ark, and indeed many youngsters will never have used a free-line—or even heard of it! But we used to catch a lot of carp from weedbeds on the method. A lot of the problems associated with fishing in weed disappear completely when we dispense with the lead.

The bait, which may be a large paste-bait, or golfball size boilie, is simply cast into the weed and allowed to settle where it will. It will not necessarily reach the bottom, of course, but that does not matter.

One of the main difficulties associated with free-lining is the bellying of the line that occurs in a cross-wind. This can drag the bait out of position. If the line on the reel-spool is "painted" with dilute washing-up liquid prior to casting, it will sink much more readily and the effects of bellying thus minimised.

An alternative, and one that will appeal more to those who cannot come to terms with a leadless end-tackle, is to use a very long hook-link. Although the lead buries itself in the weed, the long hook-link enables a slow-sinking bait to settle gently on top (Fig 27). There is no point making this a running lead, it would not work as such in the weed, so it might as well be fixed. A long HPPE link is prone to tangling, so mono is better. Alternatively an HPPE link can be stiffened with anti-tangle gel.

A neutral-density boilie is good for this method, as is a critically-balanced pop-up, or piece of balanced floater-cake. The bait can either enclose the hook completely, as with the freeline method just described, or it can be fished bolt-rig or short-hair style. Ideally the hook-point should be encased in PVA to prevent it becoming hung-up as it sinks. In truth I have used this technique more for tench than I have for carp, but I assure you it works.

In the Carp Society's Tenth Anniversary issue of *Carp Fisher*, there was an article by Kevin Nash in which he described his experiences on

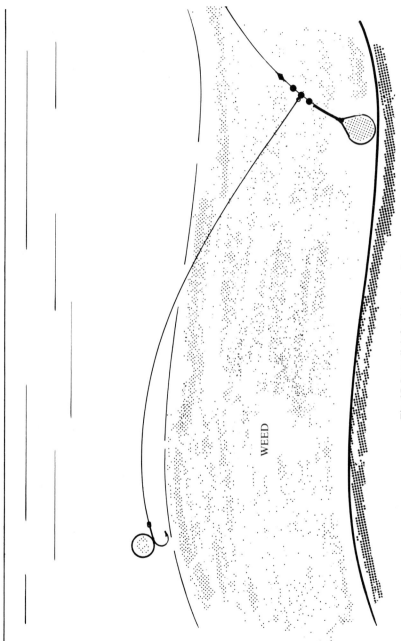

WEED

Fig. 27. Long-link fixed-lead weed-rig.

a weedy Cambridgeshire lake. Kevin tried the long-tail arrangement, such as I have just described, but concluded that it was not working very well because he encountered too many line pick-ups and rod-top knocks. He therefore developed a special version of the rotary rig whereby the hook-link was free to ride up the line to a pre-determined extent. The weed in the lake was about three feet deep so Kevin set his stop-knot at three and a half feet (Fig 28), which enabled him to present his critically balanced boilie on top of the weed. On paper it looks an elegant arrangement; but does it work? Kevin's 28 carp in a day and a half, including 17 doubles, topped by a twenty-plus, suggests so! I have only tried it once, and that was while fishing an horrendously weeded lake for tench. My swim was nearly 20 feet deep, and weed grew from bottom to about mid-depth. I set the stop-knot at 10 feet, and whilst I did not catch anything, I was able to demonstrate to myself that the rig was successful in presenting the bait effectively.

I do not normally write about rigs that I have not used extensively; but weed fishing presents so many problems, and there are so few effective solutions, that I decided to break my rule and offer Kevin's arrangement for your consideration.

Like most good ideas it is simple; and on seeing it described in Kevin's article I thought it was so blindingly obvious that I wondered why I had not thought of it!

Nice one, Kevin!

Whatever method you choose, you **must** have faith in it. If you are casting to a clear spot, do **not** be tempted to give it a little tug to check that it is not weeded. Once you start doing that, the maggot of doubt will erode your confidence, and you will spend all your time re-casting. I know. I've been there and done it!

For the same reason, do not allow yourself to think, "I bet that tangled. I'd better retrieve and check that it is okay . . ."

What is needed is positive thought.

Easier said than done! Many times I have cast out in such situations, and spent the next half hour fighting the temptation to retrieve and check that everything is all right.

Sometimes I succumb.

I psych myself up to dispel my doubts and be "laid-back" after the next cast. The tackle lands, and as I gaze at the spreading rings I think, "That looked a tiny bit to the left of where I want it . . . but no, I'm going to leave it! On the other hand, if it **is** buried in weed I'm wasting my time sitting here . . . perhaps I'll just give it a little tug . . ."

See what I mean?

Contrary to popular belief, and the impression given in articles and books, even angling writers suffer the torment of self-doubt. This one does, anyway!

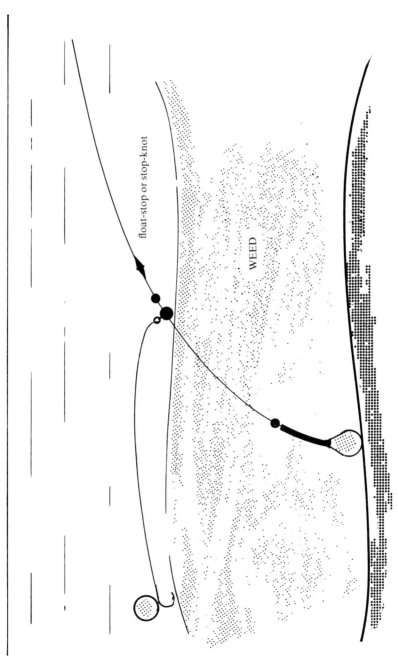

float-stop or stop-knot

WEED

Fig. 28. Kevin Nash's version of the rotary-rig for fishing over weed.

I wish I could be like one friend of mine, a particle specialist, who manages to be the easy side of "laid-back". He uses standard leger-rigs, and does not worry whether they land in weed or not. His philosophy is, "If they want it badly enough, they'll find it".

Now **that** is positive thinking!

He catches his share of carp, from very weedy waters too; so perhaps he is right and the rest of us worry too much.

The final possibility, and one that works well no matter how weedy the water, is to use surface baits. Floater fishing is not specifically a weed-beating method, but by its nature works well.

IS IT WORTH IT?

The "nightmare scenario", as the Americans would say, is a very large, deep water with extensive weed growing in all areas that are less than about 18 feet. Deeper spots are not affected by rooted weed, but many are covered with tackle-clogging blanket weed.

As if the physical problems are not bad enough, the water holds very few carp.

So how do we locate carp in a water such as that?

Most of the time, we don't!

Trouble is, carp do not move about much in weedy waters. Why should they? They can spend their days and nights in a secure, food-rich sanctuary, so why on earth should they roar around the water in response to changes of wind direction or temperature? Not that wind has as much effect on a weedy water as it does on a weedfree one—the weed restricts water movement and inhibits the development of sub-surface currents.

Given a 30 acre water with, say, five of those acres weeded; it is a reasonable bet that carp will be drawn to the weeded area. But where do you look if virtually all 30 acres are weeded?

In short, weedy-water carp can be **very** difficult to find.

But our difficulties do not end there. Carp cannot find food so readily by sight and touch in thick weed, so they can be unaware of a bait even though it may be very close by. And if they do find it, the weed may so adversely affect presentation that they do not, or cannot, pick it up.

No wonder such waters are among the most difficult around.

And if, against all the odds, a carp is actually hooked; there is the problem of extracting it from an underwater jungle.

All of which makes me wonder why I spend so much time on waters of this type!

Am I a masochist, or just plain stupid? Certainly not the former, but perhaps the latter. But mainly it is because big, difficult, problematical waters do not attract many anglers; so whereas I may not catch much, it is enjoyable failure!

With my hand on my heart, I can say that I would rather fail among the buttercups, than succeed among the bivvies.

Just occasionally though, I succeed among the buttercups. Success does not have to come in the form of an enormous fish, either—a double figure carp can have me practically doing cartwheels!

11 Winter Through Spring

Recently, on a dull, cold late December day, I had a guest-trip on a very shallow estate lake with Brian Mills. I fished to an island, casting to the edge of the overhanging rhododendrons. It was a classic winter spot, and although I had a couple of jerky takes, almost certainly from small carp, I caught nothing. Brian fished a very shallow backwater choked with dying lily stalks and "cabbages"; another classic winter spot. He caught five!

Yes, they were small, but as his catch represented five-sixths of the total carp-catch on the water that day, he was obviously doing something right. The "something" in this instance was freelining with tiny pieces of luncheon-meat and breadflake, right in among the weeds. Most of his fish took on the drop.

I relate that little account to point out that whilst winter fishing can be a very specialised branch of the sport; a good angler using very basic methods, can sometimes outfish those using sophisticated baits and rigs.

So when I or anyone else tells you that it is usually necessary to use this method and that bait, remember that there is always someone like Brian who will disprove the "rule".

As well as the two typical swims already described, there is a tendency for winter fish to move to deeper water. This is relative, in that it happens on both shallow and deep waters. There does not seem to be an optimum winter depth that carp will seek.

They are attracted to features and snags too. This is particularly noticeable in rivers and canals, where bridges, sluices and mooring-posts all seem to appeal.

Because winter fish do not move about as much as they do in summer and autumn, they seem to choose spots that are likely to guarantee a fairly undisturbed existence. In some waters this might be somewhere quite a long way from the bank, or adjacent to an inaccessible island.

This may not apply to rivers and canals, because the combination of flow and boat-traffic ensures fairly constant disturbance. But if quiet spots such as backwaters, bays and disused arms are available, carp will

I cast to the edge of the rhododendrons.

move into them.

Weather conditions for winter fishing are something about which I constantly keep changing my mind. At one time I would have said that big, mild winds were best. And whilst it is true that some of my best catches have come on such days, I cannot honestly say that the fishing has been anything like consistent or predictable. Sometimes, in fact, results can be unexpectedly good when conditions look most unpromising. Recently, for example, I fished on a day when an overnight frost was followed by a strong wind that felt as though it came equipped with scalpels! I expected to blank, but had five runs, landing four, and losing one in snags.

The following weekend there was thick fog. A friend, Dennis Holding, and I did not rate our chances at all; at times it was so thick that we lost sight of our terminal tackles as we cast. I caught three carp; the first I have ever taken in such conditions.

Next weekend it was milder, and a nice mellow wind blew. I expected to catch, and did—but did not do as well as I expected. I took a couple.

Then came the nicest weekend of them all; sunny, mild and really pleasant. Quite untypical for December. Dennis scratched one out; I

Fog; only once have I caught carp under such conditions.

blanked.

I could give many other examples, but the few I have quoted serve to illustrate my point that it is very difficult to predict accurately how winter carp will behave. Sometimes they feed when we least expect them to, and fail to do so when we anticipate doing well. Perhaps Rick is right when he says the best policy is to fish whenever the water is bendy!

The question of feeding times is a confusing one too. Or is it? We accept that different waters produce at varying times in summer; why should it be any different in winter? Some waters fish well in the daytime, some produce better at night. In general, though, winter feeding seems to be more accurately timetabled than it does in summer. No, that is not quite true. I can think of lots of examples of "timetable" feeding in summer as well, but it does not seem so rigid as it tends to be in winter.

On any given winter water there will usually be one or two quite brief feeding times in a 24 hour period, and these can duplicate with uncanny accuracy on successive days. But it changes. A water I have been fishing this winter gave a nice demonstration of this, when the November feeding times of 9.00 am, midday and 2.00 pm switched, by mid-December, to 3.00 pm and dusk.

I am currently convinced that milk-protein baits work best in winter. I know some anglers use bird-foods with success, and as time goes on I may be persuaded to do likewise; but at present I am happiest with a milk-protein mix. I do not, however, use many freebies; often I will fish hook-baits alone, or with just a one or two bait stringer. If I do put out freebies, it is unlikely that it will be more than four or five round each hook bait.

Carp do not have to be weaned onto a winter milk-protein bait; I believe it has its own inherent attraction. I further believe that the attraction is instant in cold water, and requires no prebaiting.

Current received wisdom is that fish-meals are ineffective in winter. I suspect this is to do with the fact that fish-meal baits tend to be fished among a lot of freebies. This, as a basic strategy, rarely works in winter, with any sort of bait. Before I became a milk-protein convert I caught a lot of winter carp on baits containing quite a significant proportion of fish-meal; but I used them as hook-bait only or, at most, with just a few free samples.

I have never caught a winter carp on floating baits, but I know that some have done so successfully. Several years ago Chris Currie wrote some articles about winter fishing with Chum Mixers. He expressed the opinion that providing fish were weaned on Mixers during the warmer months, they would continue to take them in winter. More recently, Chris Ball wrote on the subject and described the capture of a March thirty-plus that he stalked from beneath overhanging rhododendrons. Impressive stuff!

A couple of years ago, in late March, I visited a small, deep lake in Germany, after a blank night on a nearby big pit. It had been a bitterly cold night, and there had been a really crunchy frost; so I was not expecting to see anything in the small lake. My local contact, however, assured me that I would see carp if I threw in some crusts. More out of politeness than expectation, I humoured him and catapulted out half a dozen small crusts. They drifted towards me unmolested; then all of a sudden, almost at my feet, there was a swirl—and one of the crusts went down! Seconds later, another one was taken. I fired out some more, and within minutes had possibly a dozen carp taking crusts from the surface. This on a morning when the ground was white and iron-hard! They were not large fish, I doubt if I saw a double among them; but I was nonetheless impressed. The lake was evidently controlled by a small local club, and I was told that for the price of a bottle of Schnapps I could probably have a day there; but I had other plans, so politely declined my friend's offer to negotiate on my behalf. It would have been interesting though.

I do not think that rigs need to be radically different in winter, but I do prefer to use very sharp, fine-wire hooks; and if the weed/snag situation permits I opt for Owner size seven or Starpoint size six. When carp are especially finicky, it is worth trying the gelled concertina-rig to give them a bit of extra confidence, which may prompt them to take the bait properly and give a strikeable registration.

Winter carp do not necessarily give blinding runs when they pick up a bait, and a high proportion of those I catch are taken by a sort of twitcher-hitting approach. That is not to say that I hover over the rods waiting for the merest mini-movement. I am not capable of that degree of concentration, and am not blessed with the necessary coiled-spring responses. But I am capable of responding to a fish that gives a warning "bleep" or two, and then slowly lifts the indicator. It may not pull the line from the line-clip, if one is being used; it may not cause a single "click" from the clutch or bait-runner, but if it pulls the line taut, and obligingly holds it there, I can hit it. Such fish are easy to connect with; the line being prevented from spilling-out by either hooking it over the forefinger, where it comes away from the line-clip, or dropping a finger on the spool to stop it revolving. The pick-up or bait/clutch-runner mechanisms can be engaged after the fish is hooked.

One phenomenon of winter fishing that I do not understand is that although a few waters fish nearly as well in winter as in summer, most are much more difficult—and a few are very nearly impossible. Sometimes the "they don't feed in winter here" folklore is self-fulfilling; nobody tries so it does not produce. Because it does not produce, nobody tries ... and so on. But there are many waters that **are** fished, yet still fail to produce. Or at best, produce only the very occasional fish.

One oft-quoted comment is that winter fishing profits from a constant trickle of bait going in. Conversely, waters that see little or no bait are deemed to be more difficult. This is one of those comments that is repeated ad-nauseam, and becomes widely accepted as a result. It is nonsense. There is absolutely no basis for the belief. When I started trying to catch carp in winter, it was from waters that had **never** been winter-fished, and **never** saw carp baits after the end of September or early October. In those days it was widely accepted that carp hibernated in winter, and those of us who believed otherwise were considered misguided, at best – or completely mad, at worst! Even Dick Walker, who has often been called the father of modern carp angling, expressed the opinion that winter fishing was a complete waste of time. But despite the lack of bait that went in carp waters, they were no less catchable then, than they are now. Quite the contrary, in fact.

In a recent article Lee Jackson asked the question, "Have you noticed how difficult winter carp fishing is becoming these days?"

Yes, I have, and so have most other winter carp enthusiasts. But this is hardly surprising; after all, summer fishing has got more difficult too. The decline is more apparent in winter, because on any given day,

Few waters are neglected in winter these days.

in any given water, there will only be a small number of carp feeding. Until four or five years ago, very few anglers fished for them, so they were not pressured.

Nowadays, particularly at weekends, it is likely that there will be several anglers fishing, they are thus "sharing" very few feeding fish—and stressing them in the process. It is, therefore, simply an increase in angling pressure that has made winter carp fishing more difficult.

Talking of which, there are inexplicable "dead" periods that occur, even on waters that normally produce in winter—and paradoxically these periods often happen when conditions look really good.

Not that it is consistently difficult all through the winter. November is usually good, especially the early and middle part of the month. Late November and early December often start to get a bit more difficult. By late December the weather and the fishing have normally become hard. January is generally a pig of a month; carp seem to feed very infrequently, and most years we lose fishing time due to ice-cover and impassable roads. It is worth bearing in mind, though, that lakes near the coast are often the last to freeze because of the moderating effect of the sea on coastal temperatures, and the fact that such waters are often slightly

A few years ago even well-known waters were neglected in winter—this is Johnson's Railway Lake, and completely deserted!

saline.

And February—well, frankly I would not have been upset in the past had February been deleted from the calendar and we reverted to an eleven-month year! But in February '91 brother Rick rang at what became almost monotonously regular intervals, relating details of catches that would have done credit to July in a good year! One particular catch I recall occurred just after the ice cleared; he took six carp to 17 lb, and three tench, in one short day-session. A marvellous day, marred only by the fact that on getting back to the car-park he found that some moron had broken into his car.

It appears that anti-social retards are having an increasingly adverse effect on all aspects of life. They really are a total waste of space aren't they? Can't we find a role for them? ... use them to plug the hole in the ozone layer, perhaps?

After that diverting diversion, which arose from talking about February, and the fact that it is normally a very difficult month; it is worth noting the way hitherto "dead" waters can suddenly "come alive" at the tail-end of the season. In March 91 we had, you may recall, some very pleasant spring-like weather which followed countrywide snow and

At last I've got the water to myself—Boxing Day on Leisure Sport's Larkfield Two.

two weeks of sub-zero temperatures. It was a dramatic reversal. I was not able to fish the last weekend of the season as I was committed to speaking at an overseas carp conference, but I had a number of telephone calls from friends on my return, and the general pattern of the stories was of a sudden flurry of activity.

Rick rang, "Two anglers had seven fish from the shallows; their first runs all winter".

Ken Crow rang, "Honeycroft produced eight carp this weekend, three of them were twenties". The significance being that apart from three fish the previous weekend there had only been two others in the preceding four months!

And so on.

Interestingly, in these and other reports it seems that a high proportion of the carp caught had come from the shallower areas of the waters concerned. I would not say that was typical of late-season "flurries", but it certainly happened in '91.

I have never fished on the continent in the middle of winter, but I have fished in northern Europe in early November, and in very cold weather in March and April. I have caught stillwater carp at those times, but conversation with continental friends convinces me that I would be better off fishing canals. Geordie Mike will doubtless remember our November trip when a very good friend of mine came down to the lake to see how we were getting on. Now this man, let me tell you, is an incredible catcher of big carp, but is very, very secretive; so I was surprised when he admitted that he had caught from a canal that morning. I was even more surprised when his face broke into a beaming grin and he said that his catch consisted of a brace of 30 lb plus commons!

That particular water produces some massive winter carp to those in-the-know. I know the canal incidentally; I even know which stretches produce the big fish, but I have never fished there. Why? For the same reason that I have thus far declined the kind invitations by three continental friends, all of whom have caught enormous carp, to join them there. My reasons are related to Terry Eustace's comment in response to being shown a picture of a big Patshull common, and asked, "I bet you'd like that, wouldn't you Terry?"

To which he replied, in that lovely Brummy drawl, "No, I want me own".

I want my own, too.

And no, I will not tell you the name of the canal in question; I will not even tell you in which country it lies. Which, of course, is the reason my friends entrust me with such secrets.

If you try continental rivers and canals in springtime, you will find that certain stretches are closed to fishing, as these are designated spawning areas. There will usually be a noticeboard stating the fact. You may not understand the full text, but if in France, as I mention elsewhere, you see the words "défense" or "interdire", they indicate that something is banned or not allowed. In Germanic languages, anything that looks like "verbotten", means "forbidden".

Many years ago, when legislation was somewhat looser than it is now, quite a lot of club and ticket waters were available throughout the close-season. I recall that Leisure Sport's Darenth fishery was one that could be fished, and several local club waters were designated any-method "trout" fisheries, due to the simple expedient of stocking with a handful of trout! I did not do much of this close-season carp fishing because I was usually trolling off to Ireland or Scotland for pike; but what little I did made it obvious that it was a potentially good period, especially late May and early June. I have since confirmed that fact by trips to Europe. I can just about manage a week during spring half-term, but no more. As a teacher I have quite a lot of holiday allocation, but it is completely inflexible, and is only rarely at good times of the year. It also means I can never get anything other than peak-rate ferry-crossings etc. And whenever I am on holiday, so are five and a half thousand million kids! But then I do not suppose any teacher can expect much

A close-season work-party assembles—harmless enough just so long as they don't create those horrible dugouts.

sympathy when it comes to discussions about holidays!

Some west country waters are open in the close-season, and anglers from as far away as Yorkshire visit places like College Reservoir. Other well known waters such as Broadlands (Hants), Farlows (Bucks), Tri-Lakes (Surrey) and Old Bury Hill (Surrey) are available too; as are a few lakes in the midlands and north of the country. Some of these are commercial fisheries and, would you believe, have a tackle-shop and anglers' cafe on site ... even a bar ... wherein the captors of a few big carp have been sitting when their runs occurred.

Needless to say, I think such places have precious little to do with real carp fishing. They get horrendously busy, too.

Mind you, if rumours and whispers I have been hearing recently are true, we will not have to choose between overcrowded fisheries at home, or quiet, deserted waters on the continent, because the statutory close-season might be abolished on all lakes and pits that are not connected to a river. It will then be up to individual clubs, syndicates and riparian owners to decide for themselves if they want a close-season. Presumably they will also set their own dates. I can imagine, for example, that waters

Rod making—for many years one of my close-season tasks.

shared with duck-shooting syndicates might be closed during the winter but will reopen in the early spring.

The viability of all-year carp fishing depends on the pressure to which the water is subjected. Heavily fished waters **do** need a period of rest and recuperation—although I feel this could better be achieved by letting a water lay fallow, with no fishing at all, for one year in every four. But some lakes and pits get so little pressure that dispensing with a rest-period would make little difference.

We could then fish in May, which can be a gorgeous time of year. The new foliage on the trees has a beautiful fresh look. Lots of wild flowers are in bloom. The weather is normally nice and warm, without being oppressive. The main holiday-season has yet to start, so there are no crowds. And best of all, given half reasonable conditions, carp are active and feed well.

12 Home and Away

In this chapter I shall look at some of the different types of waters we are likely to encounter, both here at home and on the continent.

BALLAST PITS

Most UK carp fishing is done in sand and gravel-pits, which can vary in size from small pools of just a few acres, to massive excavations of 100 acres plus. Most are fairly shallow, up to about 10 feet, especially the older ones that were only dug down to the greensand layer; and they are characterised by bars and islands, created by the rather haphazard spoil-dumping that occurred during digging operations.

There are pits on the continent too, but they differ from ours in that they tend to be larger, plenty have acreages up in the hundreds, and some look like inland seas. They are usually deeper too, often 20 feet or more. Due to strict legislation regarding digging methods, they rarely have the bars and islands so characteristic of our pits.

Continental pits differ in another important respect too; many are connected by quite large channels to adjacent rivers. These are primarily for flood-relief but, and this is of special significance to us, if the river holds carp, these channels enable them to move to and from the pit at will. Not surprisingly this tends to be a seasonal movement. You are not, therefore, fishing for resident fish, so it is necessary to get the timing right. My experience of such pits is confined to one connected to the Seine, into which there is a mass movement of fish in May, followed by an exodus back to the main river in high summer. In late August/early September they return to the pit, but early October is considered to be the peak time for big fish. Which raises a rather interesting question; I mean, how does a big carp know it is big? I am not being flippant; it is just that it does not seem logical that a 30 lb carp, for example, should behave any differently to a 15 pounder. The difference between them is just a matter of weight, and only we see that as significant, surely? But big fish **do** sometimes behave differently to run-of-the-mill specimens.

Typical English gravel-pit during low-water conditions showing bars and islands.

I wonder why?

Those continental pits that have no direct access to their neighbouring river, still get their carp stocks from the river. This happens as a result of flooding which occurs, on average, every ten years or so. There is no way of knowing how many carp may get into a pit by this means, nor is there any way of knowing how big they are. You might be faced with a vast expanse of pit that, whilst it will almost certainly contain carp, may hold quite large numbers of fish, including some big ones; or comparatively few, and all small. It is very uncertain fishing, and only likely to appeal to those who regard an element of mystery as more important than pounds and ounces.

All big pits, whether in UK or on the continent, can be overwhelming waters, irrespective of their carp stocks; and many anglers feel a sense of defeat even before they begin. But carp in big waters are not inevitably difficult to catch; yes, they can be, but providing they can be located there is no reason why they should be any more difficult then those in smaller waters. Often, in truth, they can be considerably easier, because the fish in small waters have no sanctuary areas to which they can retreat, with the result that they are constantly harassed and pressured.

Johnson's Island Lake in winter.

I once described my fishing in a big pit as being the pursuit of easy fish in a difficult water. By that I meant that the fish, once found, were not particularly difficult to tempt—but finding them was a major headache.

The main problem associated with any large water is that there can be an awful lot of carpless acres. Those anglers who catch big-pit carp consistently are those who can, by luck or judgement, find fish. Luck is too fickle a commodity to rely upon, so I shall make a few observations that might be helpful.

The first and most important requirement is to get to know the water as intimately as possible. The best way of doing this is to make an accurate plan on which all its various underwater features are marked. That involves painstaking work with a float and plummet, or better still (where it is permitted) a boat and echo-sounder. This may not be practical if the water is overseas, and you only have a limited time at your disposal, or if it is too large to enable a detailed overall plan to be made. Under those circumstances I think the most practical proposition is to adopt a compromise, and concentrate on a few promising locations. I would choose the north-east corner and the east bank, for these will be affected

Continental pits are usually bigger and deeper than those at home—and few have
bars or islands. They tend to be unspoilt too.

by the south-west and westerly winds; and any likely looking areas such
as islands, bays, reed-spits, weedbeds etc. It might be necessary to narrow
down the choice even further, and pick within the key areas a small repertoire of swims, and concentrate on building up an accurate picture of
those.

Having acquired as much knowledge of the contours and features
of the water as possible, we can try to predict where carp are likely to
be.

If the water is big and shallow, with comparatively little depth variation, not much weed, and a reasonable head of carp, summer location
should be no great problem. You fish the windward end of the lake,
put out a reasonable bed of bait, and wait. In such waters carp tend
to be great travellers and, unless they have been taught otherwise by
excessive angling pressure, will happily follow the wind, especially a new
wind. It needs to be a real wind though; carp do not seem to follow
a sea or land-breeze with any great enthusiasm, which is something that
needs to be borne in mind if the water is situated near the coast.

But few UK pits fit that description because most, as already mentioned, have a lot of depth variation; it being by no means unusual

An after-work near-linear from a very difficult water; and one of the prettiest
carp I have ever caught.

They aren't all virgin fish; this 24½ pounder was well known and, sadly, shows
signs of mouth damage.

Few English pits are particularly big, but some are—like this 50 acre expanse where Mike contemplates his chances at sunset.

to have 10 feet of water in the margins, and yet see gulls standing ankle-deep more than 100 yards out! Many times I have seen anglers casting to areas that I knew were only inches deep; or conversely to 30 feet deep holes with a bottom of black, slimy ooze. It is **possible**, I suppose, that they cast to such spots knowingly and deliberately—but frankly I doubt it!

Modern carp anglers are obsessed with gravel-bars, and will painstakingly identify their range and width, and cast baits to them. On many waters this is a successful approach, and carp do "run the bars". This sort of fishing has a long pedigree, and was probably initially popularised by Jack Hilton, when he wrote of his experiences on "Goodwood" (Brooklands) in *Quest for Carp*. Rod Hutchinson described their importance on Savay in *The Carp Strikes Back*. More recently bar-fishing was graphically and instructively described by Rob Maylin in his book, *Tiger Bay*. Rob's description of how he spent many hours locating the bars on "Springwood", and catching big fish on his carefully positioned, critically-balanced baits, persuaded a lot of anglers that this was the only way to fish gravel-pits. Marker-floats suddenly dotted the surface of pits

You might have seen this picture before, but it illustrates perfectly how there can
be very shallow water away from the bank.

everywhere, and were used even by anglers who had hitherto thought
this mapping-business one big yawn!

Certainly it works on some waters. I remember a catch of 11 carp
to 19 lb I took one August day, that gave a very clear example of just
how important it can be to locate bars. A long, fairly wide bar ran at
right angles to the swim from which I was fishing. Its nearside point
was about 70 yards from me. I cast my right-hand rod to the bottom
of the bar (I had already established that carp were not running the
top), the middle rod was cast five yards or so to the left of it, and my
third rod five yards to the left of that (Fig 29). The bar-rod produced
seven carp, the middle road three, and the open-water rod just one.

But it is by no means invariable behaviour; and in some waters bars
are consistently unproductive, and it is better by far to fish the gullies
between them, or the medium-depth plateaux. In yet other waters carp
regularly feed in deep water, say 20 ft plus, seemingly preferring it to
shallows, bars and gullies. It is not until the idiosyncrasies of the carp
in a particular water are identified, that we have much hope of predicting
where they are likely to be at any given time.

There are, of course, some generalisations that are worth bearing

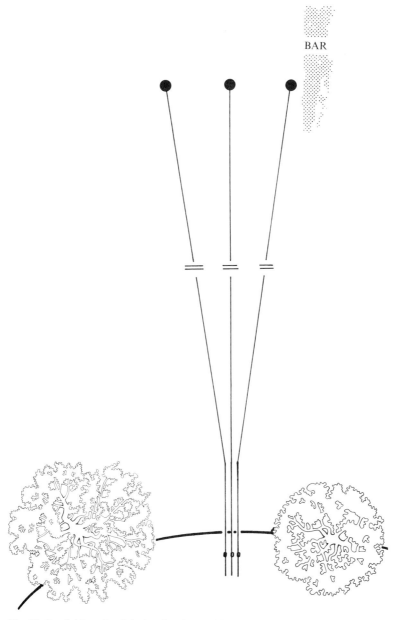

Fig. 29. Bar-fishing; the right-hand rod cast adjacent to the bar produced the bulk of the runs on this occasion.

in mind but, like all "rules of thumb", they are imprecise and should not be followed slavishly.

1. When a warm or mild summer wind is blowing, follow it—especially if it is a new wind.

2. An unseasonably cold wind is best not followed; in fact it can be better to fish the sheltered, upwind end of the pit.

3. A cool wind that chills the shallows is likely to result in a large number of fish moving to deeper water.

4. After mid-October, the wind ceases to be a useful location-aid, and can generally be disregarded; unless it blows for a week or more when I suspect that there **may** be a tendency for carp to slowly "drift" down with it.

5. When the weather is hot, fish are likely to be on the shallows, say less than six feet; or in the margins, especially if there are overhanging trees, reed-beds etc.

6. In autumn and winter, carp become less nomadic and will usually assemble in deeper areas, especially if these are sheltered to an extent from the cold north or north-east winds. They may also group-up in areas of decaying weed, reeds and lilies.

7. Carp seem to be drawn to snags, this at all times of the year. So if there are rocks, submerged trees, or sunken machinery left-over from when the pit was being worked, there is every likelihood that carp will be found among them.

8. Weeds are an attraction too, especially in relatively weed-free waters. By that I mean, if you have a big, barren water with just a few weedbeds, there will almost certainly be semi-resident fish nearby. The weeds will receive regular visits from other groups of carp too.

Thus far I have said nothing about direct observation. Whilst it is obviously the most reliable guide of all, and it is true to say that if carp are jumping, head-and-shouldering or rolling in an area, that area has got to be worth fishing; it is also true to say that in some big waters carp stubbornly refuse to show themselves. In those circumstances we are forced to rely on our ability to marry prevailing weather conditions with our knowledge of the water; and hopefully come up with a correct conclusion.

But even in waters where carp do show by leaping and etc, it pays to watch them for a while before setting up. I have noticed that big-pit carp often become very extrovert and show freely whilst they are moving from one area to another or, more significantly, just as they are about to move. Geordie Mike and I had a classic example of this a couple of seasons back when we were fishing a big, working gravel-pit. We had been in our swims since dawn but had not seen a thing. As indeed we had seen nothing for our previous three days on the water. We were desperate for an encouraging sign, so when about mid-morning I saw a very big fish heave itself out of the water, I told Mike. As he scanned the area to which I had pointed, it jumped again. It was much too far to cast to, so we just watched and waited to see if any other fish showed. Sure enough, about 15 minutes later, another one jumped. Then another. Soon we saw fish jumping every minute or two, and judging from their varied size, and the large area over which the jumping was occurring, there were quite a lot of fish in the group. They were way out of reach, but it soon became evident that the group was moving left, and towards us—if they continued on that course, they would fall within casting range a hundred yards or so further down our bank. I quickly upped-sticks and moved; and put out a couple of very long lines to try to intercept them. Unfortunately it did not work. Whether the carp arrived at the predicted spot, I do not know. They stopped showing; and where they went subsequently, I have no idea.

Hands up all those who thought that story was going to end in the capture of a "whacker"! But carp fishing is rarely like that—although those of us who write articles and books sometimes inadvertently give the impression that we succeed every time. We do not; no one does. But that example did not need to end in success to illustrate my point that jumping fish are often moving fish; and all that is achieved by casting to where they last showed, is to put baits where they **were**.

If, however, the jumping is confined to one area, it can be a very different matter. It may not—but it can be. Summer before last, for example, Rick and I were fishing a long, narrowish pit of approximately 35 acres, on a very dour day. The surface was occasionally ruffled by barely perceptible convection-breezes, but they never lasted more than a few minutes. It was a day of unrelenting sun, and nothing moved. In the evening the water became very still, just like the proverbial sheet of glass. Then way down the far end of the pit, probably half a mile from me, I saw movement. Scanning the disturbance with binoculars revealed surface activity that looked as though it could be carp. As I watched I realised that the activity was confined to a football-pitch size area. While I debated in my mind whether or not I ought to move, I saw Rick, who was fishing the opposite bank to me, packing up at a rate of knots. Ten minutes or so after disappearing behind some far-bank bushes, he emerged in a pitch that would give him good coverage of the area. I considered the rapidly fading light, and thought that if he were lucky he might just manage a fish before we had to pack up at dusk ... barely had the thought formed in my mind, when I noticed him in what looked very much like a fish-playing stance! Binoculars confirmed the observation. He subsequently told me that as soon as he realised that the carp were not en-route for somewhere else, he decided to make a rapid pitch change. On arriving in the new spot he quickly put out a stringer and, whilst baiting-up the second rod, had a run on the first! In the space of little more than half an hour he hooked two carp, one of which was landed, the other being lost in some snags. A shame about the lost one of course, but otherwise a well-deserved flurry of action, and an illustration of how the correct interpretation of carp observation, coupled with a willingness to act upon it, can make big-water fishing look easy.

Big pits can be immensely frustrating places because most are inadequately stocked, and it is all too easy to be a long, long way from the nearest fish. But here, or overseas, they are my favourite waters.

FARM RESERVOIRS

With the increasing frequency of drought summers, more and more farmers are investing in reservoirs. These are quite unlike water-supply reservoirs, in that they are usually quite small, say two to five acres, and are rarely directly fed by inflow streams. They are, in effect, little more than clay-lined holes in the ground, surrounded by raised embankments. Most are deep, 20 feet or so at full level, which is unusual for such small waters.

The normal seasonal pattern is that they are filled during the winter months; and used for irrigation during the summer which, combined with evaporation, usually results in a radical drop in level.

The constantly changing water level results in these small reservoirs being remarkably fertile, and producing larger carp than might be expected.

The nature of their creation means that farm reservoirs rarely have much variation in character. With the exception of the marginal slope, the depth tends to be fairly constant. This does not, however, mean that carp will be found just anywhere. They patrol the margins within a narrow depth-band, as described in the chapter on deep waters. They follow the wind in summer, and if the wind is a nice warm, strong one, will concentrate themselves into an amazingly small area. None of that is particularly surprising; but what **is** surprising, to me anyway, is the way carp in these waters will "hot-spot". Why this should be so I cannot imagine, and I find it incredible that it should occur at all in such apparently featureless waters.

Brother Martin found such a hot-spot which was so tight, that virtually all his takes over a several week autumn and winter period came to one rod. When he told me about it, I was surprised and, to be honest, a bit cynical. So I tried the swim for myself and, sure enough, only caught on the rod that was cast towards Martin's far-bank marker. Later, Geordie Mike joined me for a guest-session on the reservoir. As he had travelled

A farm reservoir at full level in winter.

a long way, and I wanted him to catch, I put him in Martin's swim, and told him where to position his baits. I fished 30 yards further along. Mike had two rods out, so did I. And the only run of the day? Need you ask? It fell to the hot-spot rod again!

This made little sense to me. As I said before, I knew the water was relatively featureless, so I was determined to discover what, if anything, was so special about the spot. So I painstakingly went along with a float and plummet. And what did I discover? Nothing! I merely succeeded in confirming what I already knew, that the depth was identical to swims either side, and beyond for that matter. As well as there being no difference in depth, there were no adjacent weeds, nor any other discernible features. There was no logical reason that I could find for the carp having a preference for that particular spot.

As there are no identifiable reasons for "hot-spots" on waters of this type, the only way to find them is by trial-and-error. And the only way to prevent your newly discovered spot being fished-out by other anglers, is to keep its location concealed by whatever devious means are necessary. Lying is the simplest, and works quite well. If this is augmented by setting up rods so they point in a misleading direction, and using

Brother Martin plays a farm reservoir carp with the level well down.

back-leads to conceal the angle of the lines so distances cannot readily be gauged, you might succeed in keeping it to yourself for a while.

There will doubtless be howls of protest from those who regard such tactics as underhanded—but as offended parties are likely to be those to whom "location" is simply a matter of capitalising on the hard work of others, my conscience remains untroubled. In short—I reckon they should learn to find their own fish, and stop riding on successful anglers' backs. This applies to all waters, not just farm reservoirs.

I feel very strongly about this, so make absolutely no apology if I have caused offence.

RIVERS AND CANALS

In both UK and Europe carp are found in rivers, but few of ours, with the exception of the Trent, hold significant numbers. Some, such as the Thames, Medway, Chelmer, Rother, Soar and Nene have localised populations in certain stretches; but in general these remain neglected. This is surprising when you consider that the Thames, Nene and Medway have all produced fish to over 30 lb, and those quite a long while ago. The Medway fish is not widely known about, and whilst I cannot be sure of the weight, I have seen photos and am satisfied that it was certainly in the 30 lb class. There are, however, doubts about whether it was caught or trapped. How big are those fish now? Assuming they are still alive, of course. But even if they are not (and I **know** that some of the Nene fish were taken away and eaten . . .!), there must surely be contemporaries that are still swimming about. So there **ought** to be some colossal carp waiting to be caught in those rivers. Completely unknown fish too. Possibly those carp are the ultimate challenge—after all, no one knows for **certain** that they even exist.

Most continental rivers, by contrast, are full of carp. There is little point trying to list them because there are so many, but the Seine, Loire, Lot, Meuse/Maas and Rhine come immediately to mind.

I have caught river carp on the continent, but only from an adjoining pit. My UK fish, however, came from a river proper—the Nene near Northampton. In summer I fished natural, unwarmed stretches; and in winter the artificially warmed water below the Power Station.

Although my summer fish were caught from overgrown flood-channels and reed-fringed stretches of main river, the experience of Trent anglers would seem to suggest that the real river hotspots are bridges and sluices.

I intended to try the Trent because it holds a large head of carp, as well as some very big fish; but when I went for a recce last summer, was astonished to see how crowded it was. It was midweek, but cars

Sluices can be river "hot-spots", but access can be difficult. This is Allington on
the Medway.

were parked bumper-to-bumper along adjacent side-roads; and brollies
lined the banks in an unbroken line for miles. These were not carp anglers;
leastways they did not look as if they were. But carp anglers or not,
backsides on the bank make for claustrophobic, unpleasant conditions.
Doubtless locals who know the river can find quiet spots, especially early
morning before the crowds arrive; but I do not have the advantage of
living local, and there is no way I could fish under the circumstances
I saw. So regretfully I have abandoned my Trent plans.

   This affinity carp obviously have for bridges and sluices, tallies with
the experience of my continental friends who fish canals a great deal.

   There is no such thing as a typical canal because they vary in character
tremendously. They even vary along the course of their length; some
stretches being relatively industrialised and, frankly, ugly; whilst others
can be quite beautiful with green fields, overhanging trees, farmland, and
rustic stone bridges—just like the ones beneath which trolls live! Some
canals are weed-free, others have lilied margins alongside sedge-lined
banks. Some, like the Hythe Military Canal in Kent, hold comparatively
few fish, but among them are some very big ones; others, like the Grand
Union Canal in the Tring area, hold a lot of carp but most are small.

Continental canals vary too; ranging from little, rustic, picture-postcard waterways, to massive, concrete-sided channels more than 100 yards wide that cut swathes to the horizon, and are capable of accommodating big sea-going vessels.

My canal fishing experience is limited; but I have caught a few carp from them, including my very first twenty pounder—that was many years ago, from the then famous Peterborough Electricity Cut. So hopefully I should be able to make a few observations and comments that may be helpful to those who have never fished canals at all.

The first difficulty, as always, is one of location. A canal might extend for several miles between locks; so it is obvious that, in common with all big waters, it is all too easy to be a long way from the nearest carp. I realise I "bang on a bit" about location, but the biggest Big White Truth of them all is that you cannot catch a carp that is not there.

I do not know any UK canal specialists, but I am privileged to know some of the top continental men. These are anglers who are steeped in canal-lore; they were canal anglers long before they became carp fishermen. In many cases, their fathers were canal anglers too, so their accumulated wealth of knowledge is fantastic. They are, in the real sense of the word, experts. One, after generously giving me a tour of some of his favourite spots, offered this piece of advice, "Find somewhere that is dangerous, and carp will live there". In other words, snag-areas and structures that can lead to lost fish, are the sort of places frequented by carp. He recommended bridges, sluices, locks, piles, mooring-posts, jetties, landing-stages and harbours. He told me that other good spots are heavily weeded backwaters, junctions, corners and turning-pounds. The last three, incidentally, often acquire silt deposits, which may become weeded with "cabbages", reeds or lilies. These, not surprisingly, can become particularly good in spring, when carp move into them prior to spawning. I am not recommending or condoning fishing for carp that are about to spawn; the movement I am talking about occurs in March and April, when spawning is still a long way off.

All of which is not to imply that you will not find carp on the feature-less "straights"; indeed I know another continental canal angler who adopts the philosophy that as the fish are so nomadic, it is best to sit and wait for them. He therefore fishes one or two swims on a regular basis, and every so often he catches carp.

One of the most successful canal anglers I know, adopts a compromise approach. He concentrates on the sort of features I have described, and fishes a small repertoire of them as often as possible. He explained to me that he puts in a lot of time. He fishes for a few hours after or before work almost every day, all through the year. He often has a long series of blanks, running into many weeks; but this does not worry him, for he knows that sooner or later, the morning or evening will come when

Marinas can be good river or canal holding-areas; but as with sluices, access can be restricted.

he will get two or three big fish in succession. And we are taking **big** – one year he had eight over 35 lb! I will not tell you what his biggest carp weighed—it would only upset you!

Some anglers have tried pre-baiting, in the hope that they might create an artificial hot-spot. Whilst I doubt the ability of pre-baiting to do this on any water, it is even less likely to be effective in canals, because the passage of boats causes the bait to be dispersed. It can end up a long way from where it was put in.

So canals can be difficult, especially those that hold very few fish; but there are advantages too. One being that weather is less important in canals than in stillwaters. This is because boat traffic creates flow and turbidity, quite independent of meteorological conditions.

They are usually good winter waters too, because as was explained to me, canal carp do not have the luxury of lying comatose in periods of low temperature. Boat traffic compels them to move to combat flow. And if they move they need to eat to replenish their energy expenditure.

I was also told, and this surprised me, that winter fishing is best when the water temperature is six or seven degrees Centigrade. A rise

Wayward currents, boat disturbance and flotsam; not very pretty either, but a typical holding-spot for canal carp.

in water temperature of a few degrees having an adverse, rather than the expected beneficial effect on feeding.

What of the fishing itself? Only rarely is it possible to cast out, connect up the indicators, and then lay back and relax. The aforementioned boat-traffic means that frequent recasting is necessary; and the flow created by the passage of boats, and the consequent opening and shutting of sluices, results in debris catching on the line. This, if it cannot be cleared, may accumulate sufficiently to pull the lead out of position. So it is **busy** fishing. Actually it is quite an experience to fish a water that is still one moment, then the flow goes in one direction, then it reverses ... all the while the alarm is bleeping, and the indicators are rising and falling.

If the swim is snaggy, and many are, it places even greater demands. This sort of fishing is discussed in detail in the Tactics chapter.

A rod-pod is essential—a lot of the fishing is done on towpaths, and it is impossible to get rod-rests in the ground. Oh yes, talking of towpaths; on the continent they are likely to take the form of small roads, and they can have quite a lot of traffic on them. So do not obstruct them with a bed-chair; and do not lay a rod across them while you rebait!

Those rod-rest proof banks also make it difficult, if not impossible, to use an umbrella; so a good set of waterproofs are essential. As I said, it is not comfortable fishing.

Indicators must be heavy. Even the heaviest will rise and fall in response to boat-traffic and flow; but the heavier they are, the greater their ability to resist unwanted movement. My canal indicators are horrible great things that were made specially for me by a canal specialist.

Most of the fishing is done in the margins—usually, though not necessarily, the far bank. The margins drop rapidly, sometimes in steps, to the boat-channel. The cast is made to the lip of the ledge, to the slope itself, or to its base. Only very rarely are carp caught from the main channel. Do not assume that when it is cold the fish will be found deeper, because the stirring and mixing caused by boat traffic will ensure that even the shallowest water is the same temperature as deeper spots.

One of my favourite locations (which has, alas, now been ruined by well-meant but disastrous restoration work by "greens"), had a line of old mooring-posts off the far bank. These were about a yard apart, and were positioned on the lip of the ledge. Behind the post was a shallow silt-bank that in summer was heavily reeded and lilied. It was a lovely spot. To get takes, it was necessary to cast between the posts, or fractionally beyond them. When I first fished there I "chickened out" of doing this, and cast a foot or so short—and got no takes as a result. My companion, a local expert, had five takes and landed three. The next day, not being completely daft, I decided to "go for it"! I tucked my baits right beside the posts. It looked positively suicidal to my inexperienced eyes; but I had three takes and landed two carp, 17 lb and 12 lb. The third one shed the hook, just as I was about to net it.

That 17 pounder remains my best from the spot, but just before the aforementioned restoration work was undertaken (and the lovely old posts replaced by new ones, connected by underwater wires!) a friend took a 30 lb common. In the snow too ... what a beautiful picture that must have made. Knowing the swim and its difficulties, I am aware of the scale of my friend's achievement.

You can expect to use a lot of bait when canal fishing, because a new batch of "freebies" is necessary every time a boat goes past. On some canals that may only happen two or three times a day; but on others it can occur several times an hour. Very frustrating it is too. And you will learn to smile resignedly when you have just managed a really difficult, heart-in-the-mouth cast into a very tight far-bank snag-spot, and a group of canoeists appear round a bend and force you to retrieve ...!

Don't you just love them!

Not that boats are really a cause for despair. Frustration, yes—but despair, no. A take often occurs shortly after a boat has passed. Perhaps torpid fish are stirred by the passing boat into moving, and then briefly

One of my all-time favourite canal locations—you can just see the far-bank mooring-posts from which I caught carp.

snatch at a few food items before returning to inactivity?

Finally I must make the point that fish should not be sacked on canals, or they will be pulled and battered by the wake and quite violent to-and-fro of current when a boat goes past.

Canal fishing is very different to that in stillwaters and, to be honest, until recently I did not particularly enjoy it. But during the last couple of years, under the tutilage of some very experienced and successful continental specialists, I have learned to appreciate some of the finer points of canal angling. I have started to acquire a "feel" for these fascinating waters, and strongly suspect that they are destined to play a significant part in my carp fishing in the future. Many of them are largely "virgin" territory too; and I imagine they will remain so because they do not suit UK styles or attitudes. And that is an obvious attraction to those of us who find little pleasure in crowded "bivvy-parks".

13 The Foreign Trip

It is virtually impossible these days to pick up a carp magazine, or indeed any magazine that has a significant carp fishing content, and not find at least one article about fishing overseas. A few years ago it was a rarity to speak to a carp angler who had fished abroad; but now, due to their trolling off to the continent, and beyond, in ever increasing numbers, it is rare to speak to one who has **not** done so!

Most have been lured by stories of vast catches and immense fish. And most return home having not had a single run. Even those who do catch, do less well than they would have done had they put the same time and effort into their local waters.

So the first Big White Truth is this: continental fish do **not** climb up the rods.

The second Big White Truth is: carp anglers who are successful back home, will probably be successful abroad; the rest will blank.

But what about those phenomenal catches we read about, and see on video?

All are made by very good anglers—see Big White Truth number two. And many come from commercial fisheries that are heavily stocked with big fish. Imagine, if you will, a much larger version of somewhere like Cuttle Mill or Waveney Valley, but without the intense angling pressure associated with such places. There is an ever growing number of waters of this sort on the continent, in France especially; and for the angler who merely wants to see his indicators fly and get his rod bent, they are a good bet. Just so long as it is not confused with real carp fishing. Carp stocks are constantly replenished, they being much more readily obtainable than in UK; which combined with relatively low angling pressure, ensures that they never become really difficult. In a sense they are a bit like put-and-take trout fisheries, except that few carp are removed; so they might more accurately be described as put-and-put fisheries!

Some big catches have been made on less synthetic waters, but please remember that you only read about, or see videos of, the successful sessions. There is no kudos or entertainment value in the blanks, so you do not get to know about those. But they happen—believe me, they happen.

Big White Truth number three: even good anglers, and sometimes even very good anglers, have twitchless blanks; especially on waters that do not have their stocks maintained at an artificially high level.

The upside of continental fishing, though, is that there are far more waters holding carp than at home, there are more big carp, and more carp that have never seen a hook. And for those of us who have a pioneering bent, there is a special attraction in that there are more waters that are of as yet unknown potential.

This might be an appropriate time to say something of my own attitude and approach to continental fishing.

I have fished for carp in Benelux and France for at least a week each year, for nine or ten years. At first I kept very quiet about my foreign carp fishing because I did not want to raise its profile and increase its popularity; after all, I went fishing overseas to **escape** from the overcrowded UK carp fishing scene.

But the Twente Canal in the Netherlands, and a certain Lac de St Cassein in the south of France, put paid to low-profile overseas carp fishing. The Brits went across in their droves; and as more anglers went, more videos and articles appeared, and yet more anglers crossed the channel. And so the dynamics continue to this day.

Not that we are the only ones who look for greener grass—France attracts a lot of carp anglers from Germany, Holland and Belgium; and an increasing, but admittedly small number, from Scandinavia, Austria and Switzerland. Inevitably many anglers head for the aforementioned commercial fisheries; but most go to those waters featured in articles and videos, such as Cassien, Salagou, and Cabanac on the River Lot.

Most UK anglers return disappointed, and many suffer the chastening experience of having their failure ignominiously highlighted by the considerable success of Dutch and Belgian carp anglers. We may have developed and popularised modern carp fishing, but we have been rapidly overtaken by anglers from Benelux. They took English methods, refined and developed them, and ruthlessly discarded the erroneous sacred cows. In doing so, they relegated the average UK carp angler to being a player in a much lower league. I realise you might find that difficult to accept, but it is so, I can assure you. The best of the French carp anglers are ahead of us too.

But we invented modern carp fishing! Well, that is a debatable claim anyway—I have seen a Belgian booklet dating from between-the-wars years, that gave details of particle fishing, a hair/bolt-rig, and carp movements in response to wind direction!

But even if our claim is correct; it is also true that we invented the jet engine, computers ... cricket ...!

The reason so many UK anglers fail abroad, is that they find it difficult to locate carp on big waters. Most go to France, where they encounter waters of hundreds, or even thousands of acres; which is a bit of a culture shock when their concept of a big water had previously been one they could not quite manage to cast across!

Back home the average carp angler finds carp by the simple expedient of trying to get in the going swim, or as near to it as possible. Or perhaps they will simply set up in a spot that takes their fancy, or is flat and comfortable enough to accommodate a bivvy; or in really pressured waters, qualifies merely because it happens to be vacant. They then bait heavily, and hope that some carp will wander along or be drawn-in.

It is not a background that is likely to prove very helpful on a water that bears more than a passing resemblance to your average ocean! There in front of them lies a vast expanse of water, and unfortunately carp are not scattered evenly like currants in a pudding. Most of the water, in fact, will be devoid of them. So what does our average Brit do? He bivvies up (whether it is allowed or not) and piles out an enormous amount of bait, even more than he would at home, in the blind belief that these naive French carp will be irresistibly lured to his chosen area.

Big White Truth number four. No mater how much bait you put out, it will not transform a carpless area into a carp feeding-ground.

In these big waters you have to find the fish. Once found they can, in truth, be quite easy to catch. But if they are not there, they are every bit as difficult to catch as when they aren't there in UK waters!

Finding fish on big waters uses old-fashioned skills like observation and watercraft. There will be no "Royal Box", "Dugout", "Boards", or any other known productive swim to give you confidence. You simply have to get out there and find them. And that is something few UK carp anglers are very good at.

That is the main reason why so many UK carp anglers fail when they go overseas.

That and being noisy.

I am sorry if it sounds a bit brutal, and I realise that many people will be offended by what I have just said; but frankly I do not think I will help anyone by pretending the facts of life are other than they actually are.

And the reason Benelux and French anglers succeed, is that they are very aware of the need to locate carp before fishing for them—and they are good at it!

The outcome of this, in practical terms, is that you can visit an enormous water like Salagou and find little encampments of UK anglers. These have come about because someone has found fish, and others have moved in on him; and often that someone proves to be Dutch, Belgian or French!

An alternative to fishing what have become, in effect, continental circuit-waters, is to pioneer your own. There is, as you might expect, a right way and a wrong way of doing this. The wrong way is to load up your car and meander round Europe until you find a likely looking piece of water. Undoubtedly such an approach has occasionally turned up trumps, and some superb waters will have been discovered; but more often it leads to unmitigated failure. A better way is to do some research and try to identify waters with potential. It is unlikely that you will find anywhere that is both unknown and well stocked, because chances are such waters will already be quite steadily fished, by locals at least. But you can find waters that contain carp, albeit in quite small numbers, but of unknown size and where little if any carp fishing has ever been done.

It is my sort of carp fishing. But sometimes the doubts set in and I wonder what the hell I am doing there. That is the sort of question I ask myself when I am sitting by a water that **ought** to hold enough carp to make fishing for them a viable proposition, but it has little or no track-record, so I have no way of knowing for sure. I may be several days into a blank, and have seen nothing. I remind myself of the reason I am there. Perhaps I followed-up a story of a nearby river, one that holds carp, flooding into the water many years before. Or maybe I heard that fish from a nearby lake were transferred when it was drained. Or maybe I was told by a non-angling friend that when they went wind-surfing on such-and-such a lake, they saw some "great big fish jumping out of the water early in the morning." The stories would have been cross-checked, of course, and had they not checked-out satisfactorily, I would not be sitting there ... but oh, how a fish head-and-shouldering out of the water would lift my spirits, and give a boost to my flagging confidence on such occasions!

On **none** of my trips abroad have I ever shared my water with another UK angler, save for someone who might be my companion on the trip, of course. Most times, in fact, I do not even share the waters with locals; which is not altogether surprising, considering the probable proximity of waters with proven track-records.

Some trips of the sort described have been a complete blank; the desperately needed sighting to raise my morale has not happened, and the alarms have remained silent. But sometimes, while I am sitting there riddled with doubt and desperately trying to convince myself that there **must** be viable numbers of carp in the water; it happens! The alarm shrieks its high pitched "Beeeeeeeeeep", and with a heart that threatens to pound its way out of my chest, I pick up the rod and strike. When the rod hoops over I do not know what to expect, I will likely have little idea of the water's potential—not that it matters overmuch, because even a single-figure fish under those circumstances gets the adrenalin flowing. But just occasionally, miraculously, I strike into a solid wall of power,

Mike fishing a continental pit that received its stock when the adjacent river flooded.

which moves off slowly with a heavy thump, thump, thump . . .

That is carp fishing!

And they say that continental fish do not count . . .!

INFORMATION

France

France is divided into approximately 50 départements (equivalent to our counties), all of which issue their own licences. The Category Two licence, which is the one that covers coarse fishing, costs about £20, and is valid for a year. It entitles the holder to use up to three or sometimes even four rods. A supplementary stamp, costing just a few pounds, extends its validity to another département.

Licences can be bought from tourist offices (Bureau de Tourisme or Syndicate d'Initiative), local tackle-shops, tabacs, and sometimes bars and cafes, especially if these are situated near the water.

Footnote: Some départements issue two coarse licences, carp are covered by the cheaper "poisson blancs" version. The more expensive one includes pike and zander.

With the exception of a few central regions, there is no blanket close-season for carp fishing; there may, however, be local restrictions as to when and where you can fish, especially in late spring, at spawning time. If you see a notice with the words "defense" or "interdire" in the text, you can safely assume that there is a ban or restriction in force.

Night fishing is **not** permitted in **any** waters covered by the regional licence system. Some anglers have stated that night fishing is allowed in private waters, providing the permission of the owner has been obtained. This is only so if the water is in no way connected to a river system. For all practical purposes, the **only** waters in France on which you can legally night fish are the commercial fisheries that advertise the fact.

Many UK anglers choose to disregard the ban, considering themselves to be above or beyond such inconvenient observances. Others think they can play the dumb-Brit, and claim ignorance of the regulations. And many have got away with it. Some, however, have been less fortunate, and have suffered the confiscation of **all** their kit. Do your sums before deciding to take the risk. And ask yourself, is it worth it?

Another point to consider is that French carp anglers are working hard at trying to persuade the authorities to allow night fishing. They are **not** having their task made any easier by the tensions that are being created by visiting carp anglers, who are showing flagrant disregard for regulations. Indeed, some of our more helpful ambassadors have even gone so far as to get violent when asked or told to pack up. Can you believe it? There are times when I become convinced that Darwin got it all wrong—and sections of the human race are **de**volving, not evolving.

And can you wonder that a lot of overseas carp anglers, who once admired us, are now keeping **very** quiet about their newly discovered big-fish locations? Abuse of their hospitality has thus proved counter-productive.

Put simply chaps—they don't want us; and I, for one, do not blame them.

Not that I think for one moment that anything I say will change matters. The lentil-brained morons who behave badly, will not read this anyway ... although there is always the chance that someone might read it aloud to them ...

Anyway, back to the subject. Carp are widespread in France, and can be found in a wide variety of waters. You will find them in the most unpromising looking locations; most camp-site lakes hold them, for example, although, as mentioned elsewhere, the activities of swimmers, wind-surfers and boats may make the fishing somewhat frustrating. If the river-system holds them, then so will the giant barrages. And do not forget the canals. Very little carp fishing is done in French canals, but I would be willing to bet that some of the biggest carp in Europe live in them.

An increasing number of French waters have a large population of American catfish. I have never encountered them, but I am told that they are an unmitigated pain. I am also told that they do not like garlic, which must be pretty inconvenient if you live in France! I cannot vouch for the anti-catfish properties of essential oil garlic, but it might be something to bear in mind. Otherwise the baits need to be big and hard.

Few of the French people I have met, anglers and non-anglers alike, speak much English. They are as arrogant and xenophobic as we are! They are, however, polite and hospitable to a degree that puts us to shame.

And the food, it goes without saying, is wonderful!

French Government Tourist Office
178 Piccadilly
London
W1V 0AL

NETHERLANDS

There is no blanket close-season for carp; and night fishing is allowed in canals, but only in June, July and August. There may be local variations to this.

A licence can be bought from any post-office; I have not got a current one to hand, but I think it is called a Vjiskarte. It costs just a few pounds. It entitles the holder to fish most canals and connected pits, but only with one rod. A local permit (as distinct from a licence) can be bought from tackle-shops, which entitles you to use two rods. The local permit is not instead of the licence, incidentally, it is supplementary to it.

It sounds a little complicated but in practice is very straightforward, and is made easier by the fact that **everyone** in Holland speaks immaculate English. They are very precise too, I recall being asked, "Excuse me, in this connection should I use the past perfect or the past imperfect tense?"

He was a carp angler too!

So language will be no problem, unless you are so remiss as to use a double negative, or end a sentence with a preposition!

Intrigued by their gift for languages, I once asked a Dutch ski-lift companion with whom I had got into conversation, how it was that they all seemed to speak immaculate English . . . and German . . . and French . . .and Serbo-Croatian and Swahili for all I know? In response to which, he held out his hands in an expressive gallic shrug (they are poly-gestured, as well as poly-lingual!) and said, "**Who** else speaks Dutch?"

In short, if they did not learn other languages, they would never get to talk to anyone!

Dutch waters hold lots of lovely commons, these being stocked by state-controlled fish farms and selected due to their hardiness and resistance to disease. They are not, however, particularly large; most are low to mid-doubles. There **are** big fish in Holland, but they tend to be found in sparsely stocked waters where the fishing is very difficult.

Netherlands Board of Tourism
25–28 Buckingham Gate
London
SW1E 6LD

BELGIUM

Belgium, in my opinion, is the home of the best carp anglers in Europe. Do not for a moment imagine that you will go across and show Belgian carp anglers how it is done ... you may be king-of-the-pond back home, but you are unlikely to impress over there. As a consequence of the best Belgian anglers being so good, the fishing can be difficult. There are few naive, unfished for carp there any more.

Compared with those in Holland, Belgian waters are lightly stocked; but there are some big fish to be caught by those who have the time and the skill.

As in Holland, a licence can be bought from any post-office. It is valid for a year and covers all canals, rivers and state-controlled stillwaters in the region. Seeing as how it only costs about five pounds, that is quite astonishing value! When you go to buy your licence, remember to take your passport—the issuing official will want to see it.

The night fishing situation in Belgium is in a state of flux. Until recently there was no night fishing at all (save on a few private waters); then an experimental scheme was introduced on certain canal stretches whereby it was permitted to fish until midnight, and then from 2.00 am. The current situation is that night fishing is allowed on some stretches of certain canals (you will have to enquire locally), but only in June, July and August.

English is widely spoken among the younger generation because they learn it at school; but few older people speak it. Communication can, therefore, be difficult because Flemish has to be the most incomprehensible language yet devised. To see it written it looks not unlike German, but to hear it spoken is quite another matter. I speak some German, but am unable to make any sense of Flemish at all.

Those who paid attention during their school geography lessons will remember that Belgium and Holland share a considerable length of border ("considerable" being a relative term, Belgium is, after all, a small country). This results in an interesting situation in that some waters have one bank on the Belgian side, and the other on the Dutch side. Holland has no close-season; Belgium has (April 1st to May 31st). You get my drift? It is therefore possible, and perfectly legal, to fish such waters in the Belgian close season, but only from the Dutch side! And are carp that are caught from dual-nationality waters of this type, Belgian or Dutch?

It is just as well that continental anglers do not share the parochial view sometimes expressed in the UK, that foreign fish do not count!

Belgium Tourist Office
Premier House
2 Gayton Road
Harrow
Middlesex
HA1 2XU

GERMANY

A few English anglers have fished for carp and catfish down in Bavaria, but for the most part Germany is unexplored. With what was once East Germany now accessible, there is undoubtedly tremendous potential for unknown and unexploited carp fishing in the country. I occasionally see German angling magazines (they send me courtesy copies when my photos, which are held on file, are published), and clearly there are many big carp there.

It is difficult to evaluate the true potential because German carp fishing is still very much at the developmental stage.

Licences and permits are likely to pose a problem. German anglers have to sit an examination before they qualify to hold a licence! I believe it is possible for UK anglers to get one if they can demonstrate their bona fides by showing British angling club membership cards. Do not expect it to be straightforward though; the Germans are certainly efficient, but are sticklers for bureaucratic precision. I do not know the current cost of a licence; I obtained a five year Fischereischein, as it is called, in 1990; it cost me about £20 if I remember correctly. A local angler guided me through the formalities, so I do not know how difficult it might be to sort it out unaided.

The Town Hall (Rathaus) in the main town or city of the region you want to fish is the place to make initial enquiries.

English is widely spoken, not generally with the fluency of the Dutch, but certainly sufficient for basic communication and simple conversation.

German Tourist Office
Nightingale House
65 Curzon Street
London
W1Y 7PE

GENERAL

If you decide to make a trip, do not assume that you will find somewhere to camp before the beginning of July or after the end of September. Some private sites have longer seasons, but most municipal sites are only open during the peak holiday period.

Various types of self-catering accommodation are available; gites in France, holiday bungalows in Holland etc—some of these are open all year. Travel agents have details of those that can be pre-booked in UK. Or get hold of the Brittany Ferries gite brochure—they do very good value combined accommodation/ferry packages, and have gites in most areas of France. Olau Line, which operates from Sheerness in Kent, does bungalow/ferry packages in Benelux. They feature holiday parks where it just **might** be possible to combine a fishing-cum-family holiday. Combined holidays have, for me, never worked. I am too selfish, and want to go fishing all the time! For some, however, it might be the only way they can get to try overseas carp fishing.

Ferries are best pre-booked if you intend travelling during peak holiday times; but do not let that discourage you from an impromptu trip if an opportunity suddenly arises. It is possible to book passage, and all the appropriate insurances, immediately before sailing, if you go to the P and O Main Office in Dover. I made this discovery when I was due to fly to Brussels to give some lectures, on the very day of the Air Europe collapse!

Talking of insurances; you will need a green card European extension to your motor insurance. Failure to do so will result in your fully comprehensive policy being reduced to third party only once you leave UK. A few companies issue green cards free, but most charge about £15. I think it makes sense to take out both personal and vehicle insurance with the AA, RAC, Europ Assistance or whomsoever. I know lots of travellers chance-it, and do not bother, which is fine all the time nothing goes wrong ... But oh boy, do they have expensive problems if an emergency does occur!

I used to take traveller's cheques and Eurocheques, in addition to a bit of "float" in local currency; but now I do not do so because Visa cards have universal acceptance, and have practically rendered the others obsolete.

Do not rely on being able to replace expendable tackle items while fishing overseas. There are some excellent tackle shops, especially in Holland and Belgium, but more commonly there is limited availability of many of the things we need. It is therefore necessary to take everything you are likely to need—and do not underestimate how much line and how many leads you will go through if you are fishing a rocky, snaggy river or barrage.

In the past I have either arranged freezer access, or made up my bait daily. In future I shall rely completely on dried baits. They catch fish, and present no problems with regard to keeping them fresh. Most carp anglers seem to take shelf-life baits—and as I have never made a direct comparison between them and my dried baits, I have no way of knowing if they are better or worse. I only know that I fish dried baits with far more confidence than I could the preserved variety.

As regards amount; it is no different to UK—sometimes it pays to use a lot, other times light baiting works best. As a very rough-and-ready guide, for the sort of waters I fish, I like to have about a kilo of boilies per day in summer. Although I might want more if I am fishing a river or canal. Were I to fish places like Salagou, where there are evidently very large shoals of carp, I would doubtless have to take far more.

In late winter, early spring and late autumn, I would take only about half a kilo per day. Again, upping it somewhat if I intended fishing a river or canal.

Most trips I have taken an inflatable across (we are talking a boat, here—not Sexy Sue or similar!). It has generally remained unused. Were I to want to put out a big bed of particles at long-range, I might find more use for one; but generally I rely on boilies, and can get freebies as far as I can cast anyway. I do not, incidentally, use a boat to take out my terminal-tackles. I have an old-fashioned notion that casting is one of the basic angling skills we need to acquire. If fish are out of casting range, I do not fish for them. Instead I try to find some that are within casting range.

I have similar views about echo-sounders. Modern sounders are incredible bits of kit and can evidently distinguish between fish, and general underwater dross and debris. They can seemingly be used as fish-finders. How effective they are in this respect, I do not know. My sounder, now alas retired because it did not like water (!) and died on me, was not that sophisticated, and was merely used as an electronic plummet.

This strikes me as the proper way to use a sounder; and when I buy a replacement, it will again be a basic model. The information thus gleaned is then married to whatever knowledge I think I possess regarding carp behaviour. On the big, deep waters, there is no denying that an echo-sounder speeds-up the job of mapping, and for that reason is an asset.

USEFUL PHRASES

I have commented on the fluency or otherwise with which English is spoken in the main European countries visited by UK carp anglers. But perhaps we ought to make an effort and try to communicate in **their** language? As a start, I would like to suggest the following:

If you are trying to evaluate the potential of an unfamiliar water in France you might try:

"Excusez moi, il y a des carpes grandes dans cet etang?" (Excuse me, are there big carp in this lake?).

Or if you are in a German-speaking country, and you find someone fishing in your prebaited pitch, you might feel disposed to say:

"Entschuldigen sie, diese ist meinen Fängen plätz."
(Excuse me, this is my swim).

Unless, that is, you are a refugee from the Colne Valley, in which case the following might be more accurate:

"Fängen sie dort, und sie sind tot, mein Sohn."
(Fish there, and you are **dead**, my son!)

14 Reference Section

We are all in a somewhat betwixt-and-between state at the moment as regards measures of different kinds. At one time it was all so simple; we used imperial measures, and that was that. Recent years, however, have seen the introduction of metric measures, and we are all a bit schizoid as a result! Some things lend themselves to imperial measurements, some things more readily lend themselves to metric measurements. Common usage comes into it too, as does familiarity.

The outcome of all this is that I tend to refer to hook-link lengths in inches, but hair lengths in millimetres. Which is illogical, when you think about it, but seems to be readily understood. I talk of rod-lengths in feet, casting distances in yards, fish weights in pounds; and bait ingredients in kilos, ounces or millilitres, depending on quantity. Temperature still seems easier to relate to when expressed in Fahrenheit; unless it is below freezing point, whereupon Centigrade makes more sense. Wind-speeds I think of in terms of miles per hour, I think of distances in miles too—unless I am on the continent, when I automatically switch into kilo-metres mode! Depths make far more sense in feet than they do in metres.

All of which is very confusing! But, I suspect, makes me fairly typical.

Some current publications follow every imperial measurement with its bracketed metric equivalent. You know the sort of thing . . . "I generally use a rod of 12 feet (3.66 m), but find one of 11 feet (3.35 m) useful when I am fishing beneath a canopy of trees. Many anglers prefer one of 13 feet (3.96 m)" . . . etc.

It is clumsy is it not? I can understand why publishers feel compelled to adopt that policy, but it makes for a laboured, disjointed text. And anyway, does talking of a 3.96 m rod mean **anything** to **anyone**? Would you know that a 3.81 m rod is a 12½ footer? If not, why bother to describe it as such? So to heck with current publishing convention, I have used measures in the form in which I think they are most readily understood. Only when I think it is appropriate have I given bracketed equivalents.

In the interests of completeness, however, I feel it is necessary to provide conversion charts—so these form the first part of this reference section.

All metric measurements are corrected to two decimal places.

LENGTH

inches	centimetres
1	2.54
2	5.08
3	7.62
4	10.16
5	12.7
6	15.24
7	17.78
8	20.32
9	22.86
10	25.40
11	27.94
12	30.48

To go beyond this point: multiply inches by 2.54 to convert to centimetres; and divide centimetres by 2.54 to convert to inches.

feet	metres
1	0.3
2	0.61
3	0.91
4	1.22
5	1.52
6	1.83
7	2.13
8	2.44
9	2.74
10	3.05
11	3.35
12	3.66
13	3.96
14	4.27
15	4.57
16	4.88
17	5.18
18	5.49
19	5.79
20	6.1

To convert feet to metres, multiply by 0.3048; to convert metres to feet, divide by 0.3048

miles to kilometres, multiply by 1.6093
kilometres to miles, divide by 1.6093

WEIGHT

ounces/pounds	grams/kilos
¼ oz	7 g
½ oz	14 g
¾ oz	21 g
1 oz	28 g
2 oz	56 g
3 oz	85 g
4 oz	113 g
5 oz	141 g
6 oz	170 g
7 oz	198 g
8 oz	226 g
9 oz	255 g
10 oz	283 g
11 oz	311 g
12 oz	340 g
13 oz	368 g
14 oz	396 g
15 oz	425 g
1 lb	425 g
2 lb	907 g
3 lb	1.36 kg
4 lb	1.81 kg
5 lb	2.27 kg
6 lb	2.72 kg
7 lb	3.18 kg
8 lb	3.63 kg
9 lb	4.08 kg
10 lb	4.54 kg
20 lb	9.07 kg
30 lb	13.61 kg
40 lb	18.14 kg
50 lb	22.68 kg

To use this chart, add appropriate figures. If, for example, you want to convert 23¼ lb to kilos, or kilos and grams, we can do so as follows:

20 lb = 9.07 kg
3 lb = 1.36 kg
4 oz = 0.11 kg
_____
10.54 kg or 10 kg 540 g

Alternatively:
ounces to grams, multiply by 28.35
grams to ounces, divide by 28.35
pounds to kilos, multiply by 0.45
kilos to pounds, divide by 0.45

CAPACITY

gallons to litres, multiply by 4.55
litres to gallons, divide by 4.55
pints to litres, multiply by 0.57
litres to pints, divide by 0.57

AREA

Areas of continental waters are giving in hectares; the conversion factor for which is as below:
acres to hectares, multiply by 0.4
hectares to acres, divide by 0.4
A 200 hectare water may not sound too intimidating, until you do the appropriate calculation and realise that it is equivalent to 500 acres! And that's a pretty big pond!

TEMPERATURE

Fahrenheit	Centigrade	Fahrenheit	Centigrade
95	35	57	14
93	34	55	13
91	33	54	12
90	32	52	11
88	31	50	10
86	30	48	9
84	29	46	8
82	28	45	7
81	27	43	6
79	26	41	5
77	25	39	4
75	24	37	3
73	23	36	2
72	22	34	1
70	21	32	0
68	20	30	−1
66	19	28	−2
64	18	27	−3
63	17	25	−4
61	16	23	−5
59	15		

WIND SPEED

Description	Speed (mph)	Visible sign
calm	less than 1	smoke vertical
light	1–12	smoke drifts, leaves rustle
moderate	13–18	small branches move
fresh	19–24	small trees in leaf sway
strong	25–38	large branches in motion
gale	39–46	twigs break off
severe gale	47–54	chimney pots and slates removed
storm	55–63	trees uprooted

ANGLING GUIDES

The Beekay Guide to 1500 British & European Carp Waters (Beekay)
Beekay Publishers Ltd
Withy Pool
Bedford Road
Henlow Camp
Beds SG16 6EA

Carp Waters by Julian Cundiff (Angling Publications)
Angling Publications
1 Grosvenor Square
Sheffield S2 4MS

Beekay's publication is a county by county guide to carp waters in the UK and across Europe. It lists a tremendous number of waters, and gives useful information regarding permits, club secretaries' addresses etc.

   I have not yet seen Julian Cundiff's book, but number two son has – and his verdict, based on listed waters with which we are familiar, is that the information is fairly accurate.

The matter of accuracy in guides is, of course, difficult to ensure. The compiler has to rely on a network of countrywide contacts, and has to accept their summaries in good faith. The contact may, however, want to downgrade the potential of a water, so as not to draw too much attention to it. Or if he is a club secretary with dwindling membership, might want to hype the water's potential somewhat! Individual perceptions vary too—and terms like "difficult" or "pressured" mean different things to different people. But with those provisos in mind, guides are very useful.

I have not seen Angling Publications' new overseas guide either (*Big Fish in Foreign Waters* by Tony-Davies Patrick and Leon Hoogendijk), but having long been a follower of Tony's authoritative writings on overseas fishing, I am confident that it will be an invaluable publication. Leon is, I believe, a Dutchman who currently lives in France, so he is obviously well qualified to augment and complement Tony's contribution.

I am in two minds about the emergence of angling guides, whether they be concerned with UK or overseas carp fishing. Undoubtedly I shall find waters in both of the new Angling Publications guides (as I did in Beekay's) that had hitherto been quiet, but due to having their details published, will henceforth become far more popular.

Which, frankly, is a pain in the butt!

But the upside to it, is that publicised waters act like sponges, and "soak up" a lot of carp fishing effort—leaving neighbouring waters surprisingly quiet and neglected.

COMMERCIAL FISHERIES

Leisure Sport Angling
Thorpe Park
Staines Road
Chertsey
Surrey KT16 8PN

Linear Fisheries
Linear House
2 Northcroft
Shenley Lodge
Milton Keynes
Bucks

FERRY COMPANIES

Brittany Ferries
The Brittany Centre
Wharf Road
Portsmouth PO2 8RU
Tel. 0705 751833/827701

Sealink Stena Line
Charter House
Park Street
Ashford
Kent TN24 8EX
Tel. 0233 647033/647047

P&O European Ferries
Channel House
Russell St
Dover
Kent CT16 1BQ
Tel. 0304 203388

Olau-Line (UK) Ltd
Sheerness Docks
Sheerness
Kent ME12 1SN
Tel. 0795 662233/666666

Sally Line
Argyle Centre
York Street
Kent CT11 9DS
Tel. 0843 595522 and 081 858 1127

North Sea Ferries
King George Dock
Hedon Road
Hull
N. Humberside HU9 5QA
Tel. 0482 77177

MAPS

For finding your way in Europe, I recommend the Michelin Motoring Atlases (Hamlyn). They are highly detailed and very informative. The European Atlas has a scale of 1:1000 000 (1 cm = 10 km) and shows minor as well as main roads and motorways; but if your travels are confined to France I would opt for the 1:200 000 (1 cm = 2 km) France-only version which has a large enough scale to show all significant waters.

These are obtainable from most large bookshops.

For more detailed water information within a particular locality of France, the best maps by far are the IGN (Institut Géographique National, the French equivalent of Ordnance Survey), Green (1 cm = 1 km) and Orange (1 cm = 0.5 km) series.

These are not widely available, but can be obtained from:

McCarta Map and Guide Shop
122 Kings Cross Road
London WC1X 9DS
Tel. 071 278 8276

ORGANISATIONS

The Carp Anglers' Association and the British Carp Study Group, each attempted a resurrection during 1990/91; but for a combination of reasons the endeavour failed. So, for the time being at least, it appears that it is a case of R.I.P., CAA. The BCSG is continuing at present under the helm of Jim Hindle and a small committee.

The Carp Society, by contrast, seems to be thriving. Their magazine *Carp Fisher* and their conferences are enjoyed by many carp anglers.

Their address is:
The Carp Society
33 Covert Road
Hainalt
Ilford, Essex

The National Rivers Authority appears to have sharper teeth than I expected it to have. Polluters are not yet quaking in their shoes, but I think they are at least looking over their shoulders. The NRA, shall we say, has made a promising start.

Until such times as the NRA **does** have polluters running scared, we need to continue to give our wholehearted support to the Anglers' Cooperative Association. **Every** angler should be a member. Are you?

The subscription is £5 per year. Send it to:
ACA
23 Castlegate
Grantham
Lincs NG31 6SW

TROUBLE-SHOOTING

There are innumerable reasons for not getting runs, or getting runs and missing or losing fish, but I thought it might be useful to end with a potted-summary of some of the possible causes of such problems.

Problem	Possible Cause	Possible Solution
hooks come adrift	not set properly	striker harder
	poor hook pattern	try Owners, Mustad 34021 or Drennan Starpoint
	hook-link too short	lengthen hook-link
fish missed	hook-link too short	lengthen hook-link
	hair too long	shorten hair
	blunt hook-point	sharpen, or use chemical points
line breakage	knot-failure	use 5-turn clinch for eyed hooks and swivels
		use overturn whipping-knot for spade-ends (Figs 30, 31 and 32)
		Tiny dab of Superglue on knots in HPPE
	worn, old or faulty line	test all line for breaking-strain and damage
carp pick up freebies only	hook-bait behaves differently	lengthen hair
	cautious feeding	more freebies for confidence
		crtically-balanced hook-bait

But perhaps the most common problem is quite simply that of no runs occurring? There are five essential elements that must be right if takes are to come our way:

1. We must be in the right place
2. We must fish at the right time
3. We must use the right bait
4. We must achieve effective presentation
5. We must not scare fish

If we get any of those wrong, particularly the first of them, there is little likelihood of success. Get any combination wrong, and there is no hope at all.

Successful carp anglers are those who manage reasonably consistently to get all five elements correct.

There are no big secrets, no super-mega irresistible baits, and no hitherto unrevealed wonder-rigs.

And **that**, I venture to suggest is the biggest, Big White Truth of them all.

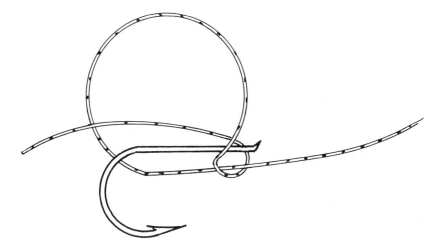

Fig. 30. Overturn whipping-knot for spade-ends tied in HPPE braid (Stage one).

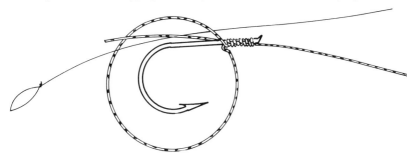

Fig. 31. Overturn whipping-knot (Stage two). Make ten turns, then pull on the main-line to tighten. I pass the silk-hair through the last loop before final tightening.

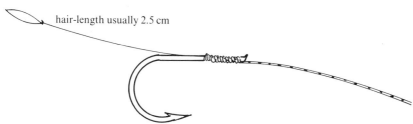

hair-length usually 2.5 cm

Fig. 32. Overturn whipping-knot (Stage three). After pulling knot-coils tight, adjust hair-length and secure with whipping-knot. Finish main-knot and hair-whipping with tiny dab of Superglue.

You will have seen this 32½ lb common before, it is the *Big-Water Carp* cover fish—but it's worth showing again! One of the occasions when fortune shone and I got it right.